Business Renewal through Ancestral Wisdom

The Circle Knowledge of the past comes forward to show us how to create a practical and ethical process for success, sustainability, and true prosperity

Tu Moonwalker & JoAnne O'Brien-Levin, Ph.D.
with Láné Saán Moonwalker

**Outskirts Press, Inc.
Denver, Colorado**

The opinions expressed in this manuscript are solely the opinions of the author and do not represent the opinions or thoughts of the publisher. The author represents and warrants that s/he either owns or has the legal right to publish all material in this book.

Business Revolution through Ancestral Wisdom
The Circle Knowledge of the past comes forward to show us how to create a practical and ethical process for success, sustainability, and true prosperity
All Rights Reserved.
Copyright © 2008 Tu Moonwalker & JoAnne O'Brien-Levin, Ph.D. with Láné Saán Moonwalker
V4.0

Cover Photo © 2008 JupiterImages Corporation. All rights reserved - used with permission.

This book may not be reproduced, transmitted, or stored in whole or in part by any means, including graphic, electronic, or mechanical without the express written consent of the publisher except in the case of brief quotations embodied in critical articles and reviews.

Outskirts Press, Inc.
http://www.outskirtspress.com

ISBN: 978-1-4327-1786-5

Library of Congress Control Number: 2008922633

Outskirts Press and the "OP" logo are trademarks belonging to Outskirts Press, Inc.

PRINTED IN THE UNITED STATES OF AMERICA

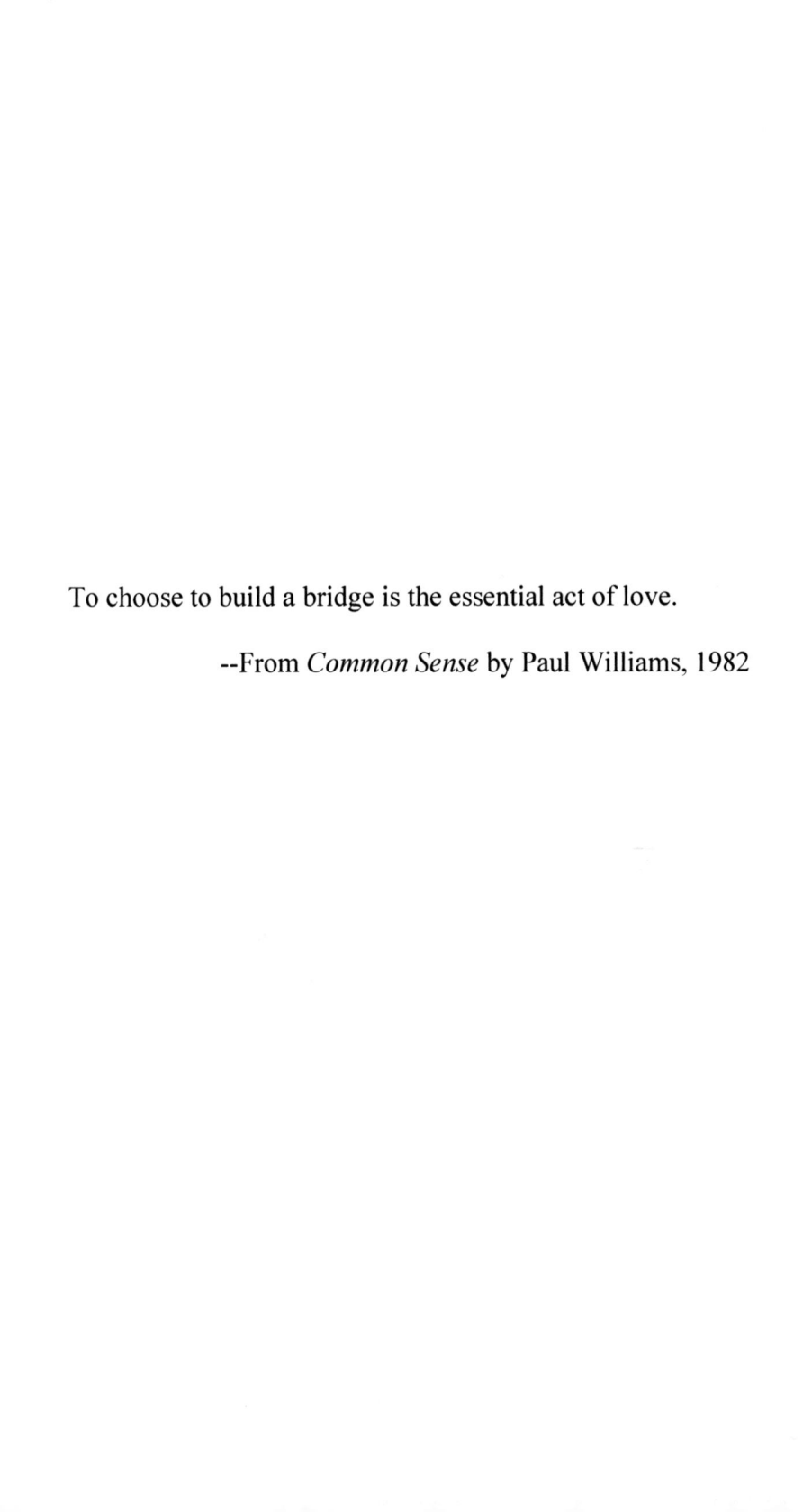

To choose to build a bridge is the essential act of love.

--From *Common Sense* by Paul Williams, 1982

Testimonials

"Tu Moonwalker's guidance has been invaluable in supporting the work of Omega Point International, Inc. She has a gift for translating ancient wisdom into practical applications. Her insights on energy dynamics have been an especially powerful leverage point for creating successful organizational development efforts. For anyone interested in being supported by the flow of universal energy, we highly recommend her book!"

--Stephanie Nestlerode, President
Omega Point Int. Inc.

"To say that Tu Moonwalker's concepts of circular energy flow and spiritual business practices work would be a vast understatement. The proof of our journey with Tu is all around us and we enjoy the fruits of her teachings everyday. If you want to bring success into your life and business then do follow the teachings!"
--Hugh Holborn, President & CEO
Holborn Creative Media

"*Business Revolution Through Ancestral Wisdom* provides a

practical, ethical blueprint that has been in practice for centuries.

I've found these concepts to be extremely valuable when balancing the human conditions of fear, greed, and hope whether building my career or being of service to my family."

--Mark Duffy, Partner
Denver Retirement Partners

Table of Contents

Introduction	I
Acknowledgement	II
Chapter 1. The Shape We're In and Why It Doesn't Have to Be This Way	1
Chapter 2. Into the Circle	23
Chapter 3. Working with Energy	49
Chapter 4. The Circle and Universal Energy	73
Chapter 5. The Guidelines: Universal Laws & Principles	89
Chapter 6. The Sacred Circle as a Way of Life: A Blueprint for Peaceful Co-Existence	129
Chapter 7. The Circle Process in Business	151
Chapter 8. The Circle as a Tool for Business	167

Chapter 9. The Circle as a Bridge to
Transformation   189

Appendix: Circle Templates for Business   201

Introduction

We need a new blueprint for the conduct of business. The evidence is everywhere. As recent events show, too many business organizations operate in ways that are at odds with our sense of what is ethical, moral, and fair. Many business practices seem to be on a collision course with human welfare and with the precious and fragile ecological environment that sustains us. Furthermore, these behaviors are increasingly costly to the environment, to human well-being, and—as is now becoming evident—to businesses themselves. Something is terribly wrong. We are desperate for a better way. We need a different foundational structure for business—one that enables us to be effective and, at the same time, supports our humanity. But is such a vision really possible?

I've been driven to pursue this question for years, seeking to get down to the root of it. My journey has taken me to all the expected places: to books and to graduate school and to experts in the field of organizational development and change. But whatever I learned seemed somehow incomplete, unable to assuage my questioning, and so I kept searching.

When you embark on a quest, you must go where it takes you, no matter how odd or strange it may seem. And so it was for me. My search led me to Tu Moonwalker, an unexpected person in an unexpected place.

I remember a moment when I found myself sitting on a hard, weatherworn and rickety bench, looking out over the New Mexico desert. It was quite hot, and beads of sweat were breaking and trailing down my face. To my right, a few trailer homes, made permanent by their tethers to concrete anchors embedded deep in the ground, sat in clumps in amongst the weeds and flowers. Straight ahead, a corral enclosed a small, mixed herd of miniature donkeys and elderly horses. Chickens scratched along in their own smaller pen. The quiet was punctuated with brays, whinnies, and rooster crows. To the left stood the mountains, purple and majestic, distant sentinels. All around: red dust, and a sky, blue and clear and brimming with Georgia O'Keefe clouds that were so high and white and grand that I wanted to cry. But I also felt like laughing. All of my searching, all my reading, all my pursuits of knowledge and education had led me here, to this unassuming patch, up a dirt road off old Route 66. The improbability of it hit me in that moment. All I could think was: How perfectly absurd and wonderful. This is how life works, if you let it.

This work is the product of a collaboration between myself and this extraordinary woman of Apache and South American Indian descent. Tu Moonwalker is a spiritual teacher. Though quite reclusive, she and her colleague, co-teacher, and adopted sister, Láné Saán Moonwalker (who is Yaqui and Jewish) teach Native American spirituality to about 200 students scattered across the United States. They are also artists. Among other things, Tu is an accomplished miniature basket-weaver, and Láné is a painter and performer. They live simply but plentifully outside a small desert town with all the critters and another long-time friend.

In Tu's teachings I found something that cut through many of the dilemmas that often arise when we seek spiritual answers to real-world problems. I wasn't left suspended somewhere in airy idealism. Instead, I found groundedness and a strong penchant for practicality. Like Buddhism, this was a philosophy that was based on keen observation and discernment, but it was not predominantly intellectual. It was born out of carefully observing what works and what doesn't, and incorporating the testimony of the evidence.

It looked unblinkingly at human nature, took stock of our foibles, acknowledged them, and then crafted a framework to help us screw-up less. It aimed to achieve this not by punishing us after the fact, but by creating conditions that supported us doing the right thing from the get-go. This was an eco-conscious way of living that had deep and ancient roots.

This perspective first developed because people had over-fished and over-hunted and were starving. They had to find another way to live or they would die. So, this philosophy also had social justice built in, not just because it was the right thing to do, but also because it was practical. At a time when human beings were scarce commodities, the preservation of human life was a sensible goal. So was the preservation of natural resources.

Most arrestingly, it looked to the natural world as teacher and mentor. It named something obviously true, but remarkably missing from our society today: When the human soul finds its place in connection with the rest of creation, it finds peace. When we are without that sense of connection, we wander, empty and hungry. We are not separate, but most of us do not know that. Or if we do, as individuals, our culture as a whole does not.

In this modern age we have wandered just about as far as we can from our starting place. We have invented, created, learned, developed, read and written our way to staggering intellectual and technological heights, but we have lost something in the process. Our heads are full, but our hearts are broken and bewildered by the choices we make. We have a glimmer of wisdom, now. We are beginning to really see what we are creating, but we don't know how to stop or what else to do.

From Tu I learned a specific, indigenous way of looking at this dilemma, this modern crisis of conscience. I learned that there was an eloquently simple explanation for the shape we're in. It is, quite literally, because of the shape we're in.

Underlying virtually everything we think and do, there is a singular pattern: the line. Despite all our complexity and sophistication, we're primarily a linear-thinking, linear-acting culture. Almost without exception, today's businesses—and all other organizations and institutions—are based on a linear pattern.

Linear thinking and linear structures have some distinct advantages, but they have some significant limitations as well. The pain that we are now experiencing is the direct result of those limitations. The line is the pattern to use when we want speed, force, relentless forward motion, narrowness of vision, and continuous consumption. We have only to look around us to see its effects. We also over-identify with our minds, which leads to even more linearity because we don't/can't consider more of the whole. If we don't change soon, we might be done for. But to get there from here, we can't just do more of the same.

From Tu I learned that a new vision might be found in something quite ancient: the Circle. The Circle is a universal blueprint, found everywhere in nature. And, according to Tu, the Circle is also an alternative to the line as the underlying pattern for business.

Simply put, the Circle blueprint is congruent with the demands of a business because a business is an organic, living entity. It is not a mechanical thing. Organic beings exist in cycles. Whereas linear structures tend to consume energy, circular processes and structures facilitate the flow of energy. The Circle can help you organize a business so that energy flows through continuously, keeping it vital, alive, growing, and evolving. The Circle is a robust blueprint with many powerful attributes. It fosters wholeness, mutual respect, co-operation, flexibility, acceptance, and evolution so that these qualities are inherent to everything we do. It's scalable, multi-faceted, and applicable to virtually all business-related challenges. It's a practical process blueprint that is endlessly customizable to the issues encountered at all stages of building, managing, and evolving a business.

The Circle is also a sacred technology that opens the door to wisdom. It has deep roots in wisdom, in the accumulated experience of all those who sought to understand how human beings should live. Historically, business has ignored or banished the sacred dimension of life. The result has been stressful compartmentalization, moral impoverishment, and ethical confusion. But the sacred and the practical are not mutually exclusive; they are different aspects of the same wholeness. The

Circle reminds us that wholeness embraces all dimensions; it reminds us that the sacred and the practical are not separate, but two aspects of living with and peacefully co-existing as part of the whole. They uphold, sustain, and reinforce one another. We must bring the sacred back into our work and our businesses. The Circle can show us how to re-weave these two dimensions into a whole cloth. The Circle can reconnect us with this sacred dimension—long banished and sorely missed.

The linear pattern can exacerbate our human foibles and frailties, whereas the Circle reminds us that human beings can be balanced, strong, and whole. By building our businesses upon the foundation of the Circle—with its innate gifts of harmony, support, mutual benefit, and balance—we can create sustainable businesses, resolve many of our present dilemmas, heal ourselves, and be rewarded in ways that teach us the meaning of true wealth (e.g., well-being, abundance, prosperity and real power). We can live in peaceful co-existence with All that Exists. The possibility is there, and the Circle can support us to fulfill that potential.

The Circle can help us transform business. As the Ancients knew, when we walk the path of the Circle, it lifts to a Spiral: the symbol—and very structure—of evolution itself. When we are on a spiral path, transformation is inherent and inevitable. If we walk the path laid out by the Circle, that path will lead us into a different paradigm for business, one that is both practical and nurturing of the human spirit. Never before has the Circle been written about as a tool for business management. For the first time, this book brings it into the world of modern commerce.

Can the solution to our evidently impossible situation really be found in something so ancient, so unobtrusive, and so seemingly archaic? This is the question I wrestled with continuously. Each time I returned with my aggressive mind and my curious questions, I left a bit more thoughtful and a bit more humble. I was increasingly convinced that, at the very least, this was a perspective that needed to be given voice. It needed to be part of the larger conversation.

I made the journey back to the desert multiple times over the course of the six or so years that Tu and I worked together on these manuscripts, frequently with additional input from Láné. Each time, I struggled and resisted until I learned to surrender more of myself to the process. This work was not just for the grey matter in the head. I learned that it was work for my whole self. And so slowly, through this work with Tu, I began to know what it means to have a sense of connection. It's difficult to put into words, but there were moments—the best moments—when I could experience it spreading out all around me: linking me irrevocably to the crow and raven coursing through the endless sky, to the violet mountain range off in the distance, to the errant wildflower. I began to learn what it meant to fall in love with the land itself. And then, one day, I realized that my sense of connection also went back through time. I knew then, in my heart and bones, that this wisdom is arising out of our collective human story. It belongs to no individual, nation, ethnic group, or people. It's the wisdom of all our ancestors. It is their gift to us.

How this Book Is Organized:

This book is an introduction to the Circle. It lays the philosophical groundwork explaining how and why the Circle can be an effective blueprint for business. We will discuss why it is more useful and valuable than the line because of its powerful and beneficial attributes.

We begin by examining the linear pattern that currently underlies how we conduct business. Chapter 1, *The Shape We're In and Why It Doesn't Have to Be This Way,* examines the strengths and limitations of the line as the underlying pattern for business. It also describes how the line interacts with our human nature to bring about effects that are less than optimal. In Chapter 2, *Into the Circle*, we explore the long history of our human connection with the Circle, the most essential blueprint in all of nature. We describe its many attributes and explain how those attributes can bring many gifts into the realm of business.

Quantum physics is changing our sense of reality. The universe is not made up of things, but of energy, as the Ancients actually knew. Energy is our most important business resource, so we need to learn how to skillfully work with it and manage it. In Chapter 3, *Working with Energy*, we provide an overview of the many types of energy that come into play in business. Chapter 4, *The Circle and Universal Energy*, introduces the concept of Universal Energy. It describes why the Circle is the best tool we have for working effectively with energy, because we can use it to help us align our businesses with the flow of Universal Energy.

Recently we have seen a breakdown in business ethics. We are in need of an ethical foundation for business that supports human welfare and honors the precious and fragile ecological environment that supports us. The next two chapters describe how the Circle can help us re-establish a strong and sustaining ethical foundation for our businesses. Chapter 5, *The Guidelines: Universal Laws & Principles*, introduces a set of guidelines based in universal, indigenous wisdom. In the following chapter, *The Sacred Circle as a Way of Life: A Blueprint for Peaceful Coexistence*, we discuss how the Sacred Circle can serve as a reminder of the rights that we must honor in order to live in harmony with each other and the world. These laws, principles, and rights represent generations of accumulated wisdom about how human beings need to act in order to align with the flow of the universe and the natural order—and thus, survive. The Circle encompasses these laws, principles, and rights, and so can support us in learning and living them.

Then, in Chapter 7, *The Circle Process*, we explain how the Circle is the blueprint for a holistic process that enables us to work with more of the wholeness of any situation or issue. Whereas the linear pattern narrows our focus and our vision, the Circle opens us to nine different energies. We can apply this circular process to virtually anything.

In the chapter entitled *The Circle as a Tool for Business* we discuss how we can apply our newly acquired knowledge of the Circle in business. We also describe the many benefits the Circle can bring to us.

In Chapter 9, the final chapter, we describe how the Circle can be a bridge for transformation. We are in a period of significant change; the world is becoming more unified through the process we call globalization. Business is the agent of that change. Because business is such a powerful connector, it has the potential to be an instrument of human well-being. At root, business is meant to be a positive, supportive, and integral part of our lives, as well as an outlet for our natural creativity. However, it's not realizing its potential because the linear pattern underlying the way we conduct business is too limited. As a consequence, the globalization process is producing effects that are more traumatic and detrimental than need be. If we begin to use the Circle as the primary blueprint for business, however, this will enable business to fulfill its true potential. The Circle is an inherently powerful and transformative instrument. When we repeatedly walk its path, it lifts to a spiral, the structural pattern of evolution.

Volume 2 of this series, intended for publication in 2008, is a Resource Book containing multiple examples of how to apply the Circle to build, run, and evolve your business.

Acknowledgement

Wisdom is a living thing. It's never complete; never rigidifies into dogma, but continues to breathe and grow.

So it is with this work. This is just a beginning. It's the first attempt to apply this ancient, indigenous wisdom to the modern business world. Much still needs to be learned.

We offer it to all who are willing to consider what it might have to offer. Your thoughtful questions and comments will help us learn and evolve this wisdom so that it becomes increasingly more robust and useful.

Sincerely,

Tu, JoAnne, and Láné

Chapter One
The Shape We're In and Why it Doesn't Have to Be This Way

Many people face philosophical dilemmas when they consider going into business. They feel torn between their values, ethics, ideals, and the "realities" of the marketplace. They believe they have to make painful compromises. The reason is that business has evolved in a certain direction. If we look broadly at the landscape that business has had a large part in creating, we see gaping inequities in wealth and power, which are getting worse. We see ample evidence that business practices can be unethical, ruthless, greedy, thoughtless, and heartless. We see run-away destruction of the environment, tremendous inequity between CEO salaries and the wages of most workers, price-gouging, and stock manipulations. Certain industries, such as healthcare, insurance, and pharmaceuticals, seem to be set up as adversarial systems where the individual customer is at a distinct disadvantage. Lay-offs, downsizing, and out-sourcing have become a way of life, contributing to a sense of powerlessness and insecurity. We also see a lack of personal fulfillment in the majority of workplaces. There are definitely good-faith efforts continuously being made to change the current business environment, but at a broad level, this is what we have created.

Why is it this way? There are those who say that all of these things are inherent to the nature of business itself. We disagree. This is not the inherent nature of business. We submit that the current business environment is the product of an underlying pattern. That pattern is the line, which is shaping our world, largely without our conscious awareness or informed consent. The line now dominates our thinking and shapes our assumptions about important matters, such as the purpose and goals of business. It is defining personal success. We can see a glimmer of this in our use of the "bottom line" as the ultimate calculus. These deeply embedded, yet largely unconscious, assumptions shape our attitudes and the actions we take. The key, then, to transforming the present business environment is to raise our consciousness and increase our awareness of these matters. We can make more conscious choices. That is the purpose of this book.

The Bottom Line, Revisited

Linearity is the governing concept of our Western industrialized civilization's worldview. We are linear thinkers, first and foremost. Here's a basic example: We think about something we want. We fix on the target. Then we "line up" all our efforts and resources to attain that goal. We proceed straight toward it. We just *know* that if we want to realize our goal, our best bet is to go straight for it and not let anything distract us. That's just the American Dream, right?

Maybe not.

Through Tu's eyes, I began to see that a line is a particular kind of energy pattern with specific characteristics. Everyone knows that a straight line is the shortest distance between two points. It's easy to see this. Just draw two dots on a piece of paper. Then, starting at the first dot, draw the most efficient path to the second dot. Now, step back and notice what just happened. You drew a line. That action was very fast, aggressive, and apparently efficient. What we don't really grasp are the consequences of doing everything in a linear way. *The persistent and unconscious employment of linearity will lead to out-of-control consumption and the exploitation of resources*—which is exactly what Western culture is doing.

To understand this, again just imagine the line you drew. In order to push the pencil to connect those dots, you needed to expend energy. This is the lesson: Anything moving in a linear fashion must feed its forward movement by consuming energy. That energy must come from somewhere. Linear structures are inherently consuming; by their very nature, they cannot be otherwise. Linear thinking is like a speeding train. It's fast and efficient, but it must consume a lot of energy to cover the tracks. The line is the pattern for fast, aggressive, and energy-consuming forward movement. It's not the blueprint for a sustainable future. In fact, the line is not a blueprint at all. It is only a portion of one. This is part of the problem, as we will later explain.

Linearity has not only become our dominant mode of thinking, it has also become our dominant mode of perception. The gift of linear perception is that it narrows our focus, so that we can fixate on a goal and go for it with maximal speed. But there is a trade-off. Any narrowing of perception limits what we can see, what we believe is real, and the range of options we have for taking action. When we are in a linear mode we cannot consider the bigger picture, or the consequences of our actions without veering off the track and crashing.

Perhaps the most tragic consequence of linear thinking is the most difficult to see. When we operate exclusively on the basis of the linear pattern, it narrows down our perception to such an extent that we *lose our ability to see or experience the wholeness of existence*. We categorize and compartmentalize. We lose our ability to see ourselves as deeply related to and interconnected with the whole. When we no longer perceive this fundamental connection, we deprive ourselves of the experience of the essential, sacred nature of the universe. We fail to appreciate the unique and extraordinary nature of each being, human or otherwise. To the extent that linearity becomes a fixed way of living, we can lose that capacity altogether.

In sum, the line is the energetic pattern underlying and shaping how we think and how we act. It has become so deeply embedded in our makeup, that it's habitual and unconscious. It's ingrained in the way we language our thoughts. We line up resources. We create product lines and assembly lines. We reprimand those who get out of line, or cross the line. Even the cultural story we tell ourselves is a linear one: The notion of linear progress toward some undefined goal, somewhere off in the future, has become our way of life. As Wendell Berry writes, "The linear idea, of course, is the doctrine of progress, which represents man as having moved across the oceans and the continents and into space on a course that is ultimately logical and that will finally bring him to a man-made paradise."[1] We are marching endlessly forward, at an ever increasing rate, certain that we are making progress—but it's getting harder and harder to say where we are going, or why. We just continue to apply linear thinking whether it's appropriate to the situation or not—because we think we must. We further assume that our only choice is to be fast, forceful, and consumptive. We're unaware of the strengths and weaknesses of linear thinking and we're unaware of possible alternatives. We're unaware that we're using this pattern all the time. It's a one-size-fits-all mentality that robs us of the capacity to make informed choices.

It appears now that we are reaching the limits of linear thinking. The world needs systemic solutions. We are constrained in finding solutions by our perceptual conditioning: the only solutions we can attempt are those that are crafted out of—and comprehensible to—our linear worldview. This virtually assures that prospective solutions will have fatal limitations. Linear thinking and linear structures have real value when used appropriately. They also have their limitations. It's now vitally important that we come to understand that the line is only a pattern and that linear thinking is not the only approach to life. As Albert Einstein famously observed, "Problems cannot be solved at the same level of awareness that created them." We cannot create holistic solutions to large, systemic problems while using linear thinking and patterns. The fault is not in our stars, but in the insufficiency of our thinking tools.

There is an alternative. We need to think and work in full constructs: the self-sustaining structures of blueprints.

The Geometry of Consciousness: Universal Blueprints

Everything that exists is based on geometric shapes. These are the essential and constitutive patterns or designs for all of existence. There are several primary blueprints. They include the circle, the square, and the triangle, as well as others. Tu teaches that all the complexity of the universe can be seen as combinations of these basic shapes.

Take a moment to slip into this worldview. Give yourself the poetic license to look through the lens of geometry. Consider how it is that these shapes are found everywhere in the natural world. Examine anything—a leaf, the human body; a flower; the curve of a wave on the shoreline. Observe the eyes, claws, wings, and beak of an eagle; the webbing of a duck's foot; puddles, rainbows, and butterflies. Look anew at our solar system, at stars, nebulas, mountains, cyclones, eddies, shells, snowflakes, and reflecting pools. See how these constitutive shapes literally litter and create our world.

In this worldview the universe is a design. It is a complex and amazing design. These shapes are the basic blueprints for the all of the elements that make up this complex and amazing design. We are all made up of these basic shapes, cobbled together in myriad combinations. At base, we are all made up of this very simple geometric alphabet. This creates a vast commonality. In this very fundamental way, humans are intrinsically, inextricably linked with the rest of the universe. We are all made of "star stuff," as Shakespeare wrote. As the Lakota Sioux say, *We are all related.* As astrophysicists now know, everything is made of stardust.

Not only do these geometric shapes make up the natural physical world, they also play an important role in the way in which we organize and think. This natural geometry has shaped our perceptual apparatus and this has a great bearing on how we deal with the world. These basic shapes are, quite literally, blueprints: they are powerful conceptual tools that influence how we relate and function. In short, these shapes shape our consciousness and we draw upon them constantly, whether we are aware of it or not.

It's important to understand that each of these universal blueprints has a unique nature. In other words, they are distinctly different structures with different strengths and limitations. Their unique nature makes them appropriate as blueprints for different kinds of human activities—and less appropriate for others. We diminish our effectiveness when we use certain blueprints unconsciously, without first understanding their strengths and limitations. If we have a good understanding of the essential qualities and appropriate usage of each of these basic blueprints we will be better able to make informed, appropriate choices about how and when to use each. We will be better equipped to use the conceptual tool that is most appropriate for the need. As we said, increasing our conscious awareness is the key to transforming the present business environment.

Let's now consider how the line, in particular, has shaped our thinking and behaviors.

The Line as a "Blueprint": Linearity and its Limitations

The most important thing to understand is that the line is actually not a true blueprint. It's only *one facet* of a true blueprint. It's one part of the square. So, to begin to understand the nature of line, we must first learn about the square.

As we've said, the circle, the square, and the triangle are the primary universal blueprints. They are the most foundational and elemental shapes and therefore the most essential for us to understand. These shapes hold powerful symbolic meaning for us humans. Throughout human history, the square has always been used to represent the stability of earthly, physical form. Perhaps this is because we see the trunk of our own physical body as square or rectangular. As a symbol, the square communicates solidity and security. This understanding is embedded in our language. It's found in such expressions as "four square" to describe the firmness of the earth, three "square" meals, a "square deal," a "square guy," the "four winds," and the "four corners of the globe." All of these denote solidity. The square has a very significant place in Western culture, because we are so focused on the material aspects of existence. We want to feel secure, stable, and permanent, and so we employ the square.

The square is an excellent blueprint to use when we want to create something that feels permanent, unchanging, and solid. Most contemporary buildings are based on the square. That's also why the square is present when we define instructions or contracts. These are generally about setting limits and defining boundaries, so that we create a solid foundation. The paper we write them on is rectangular, a variation of the square.

The square is also a useful blueprint to use when we are information-gathering. We gather information in order to create a strong, stable foundation for something we are building or when we are diagnosing a problem. If we consciously employ the square blueprint as a guide to this process we'll want to develop a four-fold view. This is what we imply when we say we want to "get all sides" and "cover all the angles." (Unfortunately, we often short-cut that process by gathering only two sides, at the most, and presenting those opposing sides as the full picture. We can see this in the current state of journalism.[2]) Once the information is gathered, we again employ the square. We store it in square-based containers such as books, folders, and file cabinets.

This description illuminates one of the limitations of the square. When we use the square to organize our thinking, issues will always have "sides," just as the square does. Those sides will be in a state of unresolved tension. The square blueprint is not capable of helping us see things as an interrelated whole.[3]

Whenever we set out to think about something, or do something, we must be aware of the blueprints we're applying, because each has strengths and limitations. In the case of the square, its alliance with stability and firmness means that it's a good blueprint to use when we want to create uniformity and predictability without much variation. The square is best suited for developing structures and processes that support repetitive movement and rote memorization. We must understand that structures based on the square actually tend to promote holding on to status quo, rather than fostering growth and evolution. That means it's not the best blueprint to use if what we really need is flexibility and adaptability. In today's business environment, we crave *stable structures* that also *support creativity and adaptive change*. Only one of these is the square's strong suit.

--Strengths & Limitations of the Square Blueprint—

Inherent Strengths:	***Inherent Limitations:***
Represents stability, solidity, and security	Limits creativity and flexibility; adaptive change does not come easily
Supports consistency	Leads to a mechanical approach: repetition without introspection and "one size fits all" thinking
Efficient for information-gathering: ensures that four different ways of confirming something are considered	Comprehensive assessment of situation may require more than just the confirmation of ideas; it may require more in-depth perspectives
Focuses us on manifesting in the physical realm	Focuses on only one realm

Inherent Strengths:	*Inherent Limitations:*
• Grounds us in the present	• Can lead to short-sightedness
• Promotes the alignment of words and actions	• Can lead to righteousness and tyranny on all levels
	• Tension is implicit

Now, we come to the line. The line is only one facet of the square. This means that, as the underlying "blueprint" of an entire culture and way of life, the line has all the limitations of the square, and then some. Whereas the square structure supports those employing it to gather information on at least four sides of an issue, the linear pattern does not. By its nature, it is only concerned with the information directly in its pathway, for that is what fuels its forward trajectory. This means that when we use linear thinking, we tend to ignore information that does not support the particular point of view that's being promoted at the time. As a consequence, our mental database will be incomplete; we won't have the whole picture. Thus, when we design our actions based on the line, the actions we take run the risk of being insufficiently informed. The term "tunnel vision" captures what we mean.

Most current businesses are built upon the linear pattern, and that creates certain results. Line-based lifestyles and structures are inherently consuming. They must constantly consume energy to keep moving, as we discussed earlier; furthermore, their use of that energy is inefficient. Energy tends to *deteriorate* in a linear structure. It's easy to picture why. Squares, rectangles, and triangles—the triangle being the blueprint underlying all pyramidal hierarchies—are all linear structures. Notice that all of these linear structures have sharp corners and drop-offs. This means that energy cannot flow continuously within them, and this affects everything. It means that we will have to expend even more energy trying to stop energy from deteriorating at these drop-offs. In general, the tremendous outlay of energy required at those critical junctures makes linear structures not very sustainable over the long-term. Here's what that looks like on the physical plane: A business starts up with a bang. Then, after a period, it needs to adapt or change (*i.e.,* it needs to "turn a corner"). Turning that corner demands tremendous effort, and sometimes the business fails. Even if it doesn't, linear structures require constant maintenance because it is much more difficult to sustain the continuous flow of energy. In contrast, it's much easier to maintain a continuous flow of energy within a Circle-based structure. That means that circular structures are more sustainable over the long-term. We'll explain more about this later.

Further, because energy cannot flow smoothly within linear structures, human beings experience these as harsh working environments. Again, it's a question of energy flow. When energy stops and falls off abruptly, as it does within linear structures, employees can feel unsupported. They can lose direction and motivation; they can become resentful or cranky, even agitated, with a resulting loss in productivity.

Linear structures and processes move us quickly, but at a cost. They have a disorienting effect on people. As creatures, we do not naturally move that fast or process that quickly, and we quickly lose our sense of context and relatedness. Let's visualize this. Imagine for a moment that you're walking along a straight line. Notice the effort it takes to be perfectly centered on the line so as not to fall off. Now, keep walking. Notice that the more ground you cover, the more difficult it is to get a sense of where you are in relation to where you've come from. When we can't see where we are in relation to the past, we lose all sense of relationship and perspective. We don't know whether our journey has yielded any resulting growth. That makes us feel demoralized and confused.

It's easy to lose our bearings in linear structures, so we'll tend to double back and travel that same line more than once. When we do, we feel like we're in the same time and space even though we aren't. That leads to even more confusion. We'll find ourselves asking, "Where am I? Haven't I been here before?" at frequent intervals. Even if we keep walking on, our linear path stays flat and one-dimensional. We essentially *never progress out of the plane we began on*. What's more, our thoughts and feelings also tend to stay on that same plane. In short, the line is a flat, non-evolutionary format.

As a pattern for human activity, the line does have significant benefits. It generates tremendous force and speed, so we can use it to narrow our focus, to set goals, and realize those goals very quickly and aggressively. But linear thinking has some significant limitations. For one, as we've discussed, it's highly consumptive. For another, it narrows our focus so effectively that we can no longer see the wholeness and interrelatedness of things. When we see the world from the perspective of the line, we tend to see it as made up of opposing forces and mutually exclusive options. This is built into the nature of the line. The line is the mechanism we use to connect any two points. Its very nature keeps those two points separate. Separation is inherent to linear thinking. Therefore, by its nature, linear thinking sees the world as made up of dualities and oppositions. We can see this in our way of life. Our focus is on the dichotomies. We live in "red states" or "blue states." Too often, our choices seem restricted to either-or, to the rock or the hard place. Linear thinking tends to breed conflict: we divide ourselves up; we take sides. We fail to see the commonality underlying everything.

The result of our love affair with linearity is that we consume a great deal of energy: our own, that of others, and that of the Earth. In order to stave off the natural deterioration that will inevitably occur within linear structures we go into consumptive addictions, such as our relationship to petroleum. We use this partial blueprint to try to create results that are beyond its capability. In the process, we exhaust both our resources and ourselves. This becomes doubly problematic because, in general, we in the Western world resist taking the necessary time and making the effort to build the kind of strong, solid structural foundation that will support our efforts from the beginning. Whether in our personal lives, our business lives, or our political lives, we tend to seek immediate satisfaction rather than taking the necessary steps to ensure longevity. Again, with the help of the line, our habitual ways of thinking and behaving collude: we opt for speed and greed, rather than considering a more measured, sustainable approach.

~ Business Revolution through Ancestral Wisdom ~

How the Linear Pattern Has Shaped Our Concept of Business

The linear pattern has had an enormous, incalculable effect on our perception of what business is and how it's meant to function. We are barely able to conceive of business being conducted any other way: it's just "the way it is." But, if we look at the current state of business through this new lens of geometry, we can see the imprint of the linear pattern. For example, the linear pattern narrows our vision so that we can focus in on a goal. Today, the primary goal of most businesses is quite narrow, even singular: to make money. The fact that success in business is defined by material gain—the more wealth, the better—shows the influence of the square, the blueprint that represents the material world.

As another example, our exclusive use of the linear pattern seems to be actually narrowing the field of those who can achieve success. Today, our economic system is increasingly creating great wealth, but for fewer and fewer individuals. Where once we saw a robust middle class, today the spread of that bounty has narrowed considerably.

The line is the blueprint for speed, and this is also defining characteristic of the business world. We want instant satisfaction and fast returns on our investments, leading to short-term thinking. Immediate results are more important than long-term effects or ramifications. Faster is better, no matter the cost to humans, other species, or the Earth itself. While there is some attention paid to the future, it's only in a vague sense. There's not much priority put on long-term sustainability or on looking at the big picture

The line is about separation. We see this in the way that business is currently separated from the rest of life—it's like a discrete realm where different rules apply, where you put on a "game face," and make "business decisions" that are justified within their own specialized context. The attitudes we assume when we're doing business can be much more impersonal or ruthless than the way we are in personal relationships. In this environment, winning over others is all. There is a focus on "getting ahead" and "climbing to the top." You want to intimidate, consume, or "bury" your competition. It's a given that the attainment of power is important. Power is important for its own sake; there's little attention paid to learning how to use it properly.

This leads to utilitarian attitude toward resources, people, and even truth. In the worse case, facts can be manipulated to support pre-defined ends. And, just as the line requires the consumption of energy in order to proceed, natural resources are being consumed at an alarming rate with little attention paid to their replenishment and renewal. In fact, we act as if everything were a consumable resource—including human beings. These are all symptoms of the linear pattern, which by its nature makes it difficult to think or act more holistically.

Since the line is only a partial a blueprint, it cannot give us a satisfying sense of completion or wholeness. Life becomes just an ongoing series of line after line after line. We do one thing, then another, then another. But where are we going? Where have we been? Are we making real progress? It's very hard to know, and that's very hard on human beings. When people live without a greater sense of the whole and their relationship to it, they flounder. It's harder for them to choose, harder to decide where they want to go and what they want to do with their lives. When people feel this way, they tend to let life make decisions for them. The same is true for a business. Relying solely on the linear pattern, it becomes very difficult for a business to maintain a sense of direction. When people who don't have a personal sense of direction work for a business that also doesn't have a true sense of direction, the problem amplifies. This becomes self-reinforcing. We may sense that something is missing, but we don't know what it is. We don't realize that we are functioning in our homes, businesses, communities, or society on the basis of a pattern that cannot give us a sense of completion. This is why we often feel a lack of fulfillment in our culture.

And now a word in our defense: When we humans try to deal with the whole picture we can become overwhelmed. It's much *easier* for us to do a piece here and a piece there, without paying sufficient attention to the whole—and we humans like things to be easy. So, in some ways, our over-reliance on the linear pattern is a symptom of our human nature. We turn our attention to that topic now.

Human Nature and the Line

As we said, the key to changing business is to increase our consciousness. Not only do we need to be more aware of the blueprints we are applying, but we also need to become more knowledgeable about human nature itself. Throughout human history we have searched for ways to reinforce those traits and behaviors we consider "positive," and to suppress those traits we consider to be "negative." This has been the role played by most religions and moral codes. If we look closely, it seems that there is an implicit judgment running through all these efforts. There seems to be a fundamental discomfort with human nature as we fear it might be, and an unwillingness to come to terms with it that borders on rejection.

We suggest that it's time to come to a deeper level of understanding. A central premise of this book is that we will be served by developing a greater awareness—and acceptance—of our human nature. Openly acknowledging those traits that define our humanness will help us develop the capacity to manage ourselves more effectively and build institutions and organizations that support our becoming the best possible human beings we can be. Developing our capacity to acknowledge, accept, and work with our human nature in a nonjudgmental way will support the further development of our consciousness.

Our Human Nature

Human beings are very complex creatures; we are arguably the most complex creatures on Earth. If you were to do an inventory of the traits that constitute that complexity, you'd see that, as a species, human beings have upwards of 100 different innate characteristics. Tu has done this inventory, and she calls these traits *human factors*.

The fact that we have all these traits in common means we have a great deal in common with each other, and that means that the potential for our achieving peaceful coexistence with each other is also great. However, our lack of knowledge about these traits tends get in the way of our realizing and acting upon that reality. Furthermore—and this is key—many of our traits are actually *contradictory*. That's what makes us so complex and what makes it so challenging for us to understand and successfully manage ourselves.

For example, as a species we're remarkably creative. That's a defining characteristic of what it means to be human. We create: we draw, paint, dance, write, sing, sew, build, invent, design, fabricate, and produce. We are the great toolmakers. We innovate constantly, making new tools and improving upon the old ones. We also tend to be very optimistic. As a species, we tend to rail against limits. It's our innate optimism that leads us to think we can put men on the moon or do other daring things that have never been done before. We also have a tendency to idealize things, even ourselves. One of the ways that's manifested itself is in our placement of human beings at the pinnacle of creation.

Another way in which we show our idealism is our tendency to aspire to high standards of behavior. We adopt "commandments" and other codes of conduct to tell us how to live, and we strive to live up to these ideals—but other human factors often trip us up. That's because we, as a species, have the potential to be beautiful, spiritual creatures, but we also have tendencies to be territorial, jealous, lazy, domineering, greedy, and violent. We have a tendency to be fickle, changeable, and unpredictable. We can use our tremendous innate creativity to destroy—and often do. It's this volatile mixture of traits that makes us the most complex creatures on the planet.

Of all the traits that define what it is to be human, the most fundamental seems to be our tendency to feel insecure. It's universal and it shows up in many, many different ways. Generally, our insecurity is repressed in the subconscious, but we all know how easily it can be triggered by external conditions or by our imagination. If we don't take steps to consciously manage it, it can take over.

Our basic insecurity is based in survival fears: fears that our most fundamental needs won't be met. Uncertainty triggers anxiety and fear. When our fears get triggered, other human factors come into play. In particular, humans crave control. We think that if we can dominate situations and people, then we'll have control over whether our needs get met, and so life will be more safe and predictable. (We fear unpredictability even though we, ourselves, tend to be fickle and unpredictable.)

Our innate insecurity has roots deep in our past, when the world was wilder and we felt constantly at risk. We only have to contrast the human with other creatures to see why this is so. Compared with other creatures, the human being is actually quite vulnerable, even frail. Many other creatures have built-in weapons or means of protection. We do not. We have no sharp claws or fangs or horns with which to defend ourselves. We have no inherent power, size, ferocity, or speed to guarantee our survival. Our bite contains no poison. Many predators can out-run or out-climb us. We do not have protective fur, a dense hide, or a shielding shell; nor do we have camouflage coloring that to help us hide. Imagine what it must have felt like for early humans to live in this reality! Given our vulnerable condition, we must have felt extremely insecure most of the time. Our key survival trait was our ingenuity. We survived by our wits. We became excellent scavengers, inventors, and toolmakers. We foraged, discovered, and created things that helped us defend and protect ourselves. We fashioned weapons and tools that mimicked the natural gifts of other creatures: spears like claws, knives like fangs, and shields like shells. Eventually, we far outdistanced our predators—and we kept on running. That primal sense memory of insecurity is still retained within us. Our inventiveness and ingenuity is immense, but our roots retain that innate insecurity, and it drives us to this day, even though we have now become the dominant species.

Toward Acknowledgment and Acceptance

We humans are highly developed individualized consciousnesses living our lives on the physical plane. We are both physical and non-physical, and we have to navigate both realms. That, too, makes us very complex creatures. Many of our impulses are at odds with each other. We're idealistic and empathic, yet also prone to laziness and even violence. We're also unpredictable and prone to acting in very contradictory ways. We need to learn to manage that complexity effectively. And to do that, we need to understand what it means to be in a "human suit."

This reality is not easy for us to acknowledge, and so we need to take a moment here to allow ourselves to feel the resistance that will inevitably come up. We'll want to protest. We'll want to say that these traits do not describe *us*. But acceptance is the doorway to freedom, as we will continue to reinforce throughout this book. And, if we pause long enough and go deep enough, we'll see that at the root of our resistance to these ideas lies the most human of human traits: insecurity.

Our willingness to acknowledge and accept our human nature actually paves the way for much hope. The fact that all human beings share these traits means we have a great deal in common with each other. This creates enormous potential for mutual understanding and peace-making, but—ironically enough—the traits themselves often get in the way of our capitalizing on that commonality. In short, they often get in the way of our acting in our own best interests. Here's why: By nature, human beings tend to be extremists. That's another human factor, and a very important one. It's particularly evident in our society today, where we commonly hear about things like "extreme sports" or "extreme programming."

One of the ways extremism shows up in our society, for example, is in the way that people seem to embrace conspicuous consumption. We just can't seem to have enough things. We accumulate much more than we actually need to survive, and those things we do have are often "super-sized." We have big houses, big cars, and lots of clothes, toys, and baubles. At the other end of the spectrum is martyrism: denying ourselves worldly pleasures and/or giving too much of ourselves. We even offer up our very lives for a cause. We may think that self-sacrifice is a solution to excess consumerism but, ironically, we're actually endorsing consumption because we're saying it's OK to consume one's self. In short, martyrism is also an extreme.

It's important to understand that extremism of any kind is generally counterproductive because it leads to a narrowing down of our vision and our options. True growth happens through the incorporation and synthesis of new perspectives, but when we take an extremist position we push away anything that doesn't fit into our increasingly narrow perspective, rather than considering and perhaps incorporating it. As we stop learning and growing, we get more and more invested in maintaining the status quo, and this makes us more fearful. So, extremism of any kind actually increases our insecurity. Can you see how our tendency to go to either of the extremes—to become either consumers or martyrs, for example—may have limited our ability to respond to the challenges of our time, and thereby increased our insecurity?

The antidote to extremism is for us to seek balance. Human beings are designed to thrive when we're in a state of balance. However, there is little in the prevailing culture that supports our achieving balance. In particular, the linear pattern that underlies business actually reinforces extremism. The line supports aggression and assertiveness to achieve our ends. As a result, business tends to be masculine to the extreme, *i.e.*, "macho." (In contrast, the Circle format facilitates our finding balance, as we will discuss later in this volume.)

In sum, we human beings are very complex creatures, but it seems we have been trying to deny or run away from this complexity. Nowhere is this more obvious than in the history of labor management. We've tried to simplify the management of humans by creating rules and structures that repress our inherent complexity. Ultimately, these repress our creativity as well. In many cases, we've treated humans like beasts of burden or machines or, most currently, numbers. We've hired very capable, uniquely qualified people and then set about standardizing and depersonalizing them. If we inspect these strategies more closely, we see that they come out of our insecurities. On some level, we're afraid of our employees' complex human nature, so we try to pretend it doesn't exist. It's much easier and efficacious (we mistakenly think) to manage a human being if we see him or her as a depersonalized number. The perceived benefit of this strategy has been greater control, but the downside is that we have not tapped into the full creative potential of each individual. This has diminished the worker and diminished the business, both. It's a fear-based strategy that generates an atmosphere full of fear and unpredictability. This then creates a work environment that is only minimally satisfying and productive. These strategies are not in our self-interest over the long-term because we create exactly the opposite of what we truly want and need.

The Effects of the Linear Pattern on Human Beings

The linear pattern has distinctive effects on human beings. It reinforces certain attitudes and behaviors—such as aggression and assertiveness—because these attitudes and behaviors align with and support the qualities of speed and force that are inherent to the line. The linear pattern also narrows our focus, so it reinforces our tendencies toward self-interest and ego-centrism.

Because it lacks inherent checks-and-balances, linear thinking is prone to illusion. It drives us to expect perfection (an illusion) from both others and ourselves. Its inherent obsession with the physical realm leads us to emphasize the surface appearance of things, rather than looking beneath. As businesspeople we want to look good, which means appearing strong, intelligent, and maybe even cagey. Going along with that, there is little tolerance for mistakes, let alone failure. The lack of tolerance for mistakes actually triggers our insecurity, which makes us tend to go to extremes. When we feel insecure, we try to control things in order to better ensure our survival. This inevitably leads to the instrumental use of others (who are, after all, viewed only as consumable resources). We can also become righteous (when we think we are right) or defensive (when we fear we are wrong or that we've failed to be "perfect").

Our fear of being mistaken or wrong drives us to cover things up, or to paint a picture of conditions as better than they are. Truth is often a casualty.

So, when we use the linear pattern as the basis for business we tend to create business environments that are simultaneously aggressive and disorienting. The atmosphere itself tends to activate our sense memory of primal insecurity, which tends to escalate the extremism in the environment. This is what happens when the line dominates.

--Effects of Linear Pattern on Human Beings and Business—

The Linear Pattern:
- Is a partial blueprint, innately consumptive and separating
- Narrows our focus and vision
- Supports speed and force to attain ends

Effect on Human Beings:
- Narrows our focus, so we can become ego-centric
- Triggers our innate insecurity and fear, so we try to control
- Inculcates fear of being seen as imperfect or wrong, so we tend to become defensive and/or righteous
- Fosters extremism
- Leads to little sense of direction, completion, or fulfillment

Impact on Business Climate:
- Narrows purpose to single goal: material wealth
- Supports illusion of attainable perfection, so little toleration for mistakes or failures
- Fosters speed and aggression: instant satisfaction, immediate results, and short-term return on investment
- Encourages power-seeking for its own sake
- Separates business from the rest of life
- Fosters utilitarian attitude toward human and non-human resources; encourages consumption of resources without conserving or giving back
- Fosters extreme (*i.e.*, "macho") business culture

This is quite an unflattering view of the business world and there are, of course, exceptions. But these exceptions serve to prove the rule. We may accept all of these things as inevitable, as "just the way things are"—but it's not so. All of these values arise directly out of the nature of linearity.

Linearity makes it difficult to slow down, to take into account other perspectives (or the whole), or to have a wider vision. This is why we can't use linear thinking to create a more coherent and humanistic business environment. Efforts to re-work the results created by the linear pattern without understanding the importance of underlying blueprints will not be sustained because the change isn't deep enough.

In sum, then, the indigenous perspective that underlies this book says that nature is made up of geometric patterns, and so is our consciousness. Each of these universal blueprints has a unique and innate nature. We apply these blueprints constantly in our interaction with the world. However, we are currently quite unaware of this, which has resulted in a diminished toolkit and inappropriate usage. The more we understand about the nature of these blueprints, the greater the range of tools at our disposal, and the better able we will be to use them appropriately.

Our current model of business is based on the linear pattern. It does some things well, but it has many limitations. It's no longer sufficient to our needs. We need another vision.

We propose that the Circle holds great promise as a complement or alternative to the line as the underlying blueprint for business. This is not to dismiss the line entirely, for it's useful when used appropriately, not exclusively and extremely. By understanding the nature of these two patterns, by understanding what the Circle blueprint offers and contrasting that with the effects produced by the linear pattern, we can begin to make more informed choices, leading to significantly different results. In the next chapters we'll explore the Circle as a blueprint in detail, explaining why and how the Circle can help us transform the shape of business.

Chapter Two
Into the Circle

As long as there has been human consciousness, there have been circles in our lives. Long before written history, we ornamented our bodies with circles in the form of rings, bracelets, and anklets. Not only is the circle ancient, it's also universal, found in virtually every culture. For example, the ancient symbol of the snake with its tail in its mouth—forming a circle—appears on every continent. Great stone circles, such as Stonehenge, are scattered across the British Isles. They are also found in Scandinavia and West Africa as well as the prairie regions of North America. It seems that virtually all cultures have circle dances. There are the "whirling dervishes" of the Islamic tradition, the traditional hora dance of the Jewish people, the traditional circle dances of Africans and Polynesians, and the hoop dances of Native Americans.

Mandalas, too, are ancient and universal. The Sanskrit word "Mandala" means "circle" or "completion." A Mandala is a microcosm: the cosmos rendered in a circular, geometric image.[4] Mandalas are extremely powerful and evocative. From ancient times up to today we have used them to create sacred space and to encourage contemplation of the universe and our place within it.

Their origin is Hindu, but they also appear, for example, in the glorious rose windows of the 12th and 13th century European Christian cathedrals at Chartres, Sainte Chapelle, and Notre Dame in Paris. They are important in Buddhism where they often take the form of elaborate sand paintings that are destroyed shortly after completion, in order to help us reflect on the impermanence of existence. The Navajo have a remarkably similar practice of sand painting. All these ways of working with the circle are sacred, powerful, and evocative.

We see circles in all the great spiritual traditions. In many, the circular nimbus or halo is a mark of spiritual advancement. In Christianity there are rosaries and holy wafers. In Taoism there is the yin-yang symbol, representing the unity of opposites and "the Way." The ancient Egyptian sun god, Ra, was represented as a circle; behind the powerful Hindu god Shiva is a circle. Islam incorporates a circle in its symbol, the crescent moon, and in the way the dome of the mosque curves toward the heavens to focus attention on Allah. The sacred kivas of the pueblo peoples of the Southwest have been built as a circular space for centuries.

The wheel is the circle in perpetual motion and it, too, seems to be everywhere. There are rock engravings of wheels that date back to the Neolithic epoch, ages before the physical wheel as a mode of transportation was invented. The concept of a moving circle, *i.e.,* a wheel, is also linked to the sacred. The Old Testament, for example, tells the story of Ezekial, who had a great vision of The Wheel: "Wherever the spirit would go, they went, and the wheels rose along with them; for the spirit of the living creatures was in the wheels."[5] In ancient times people celebrated the solstice by rolling fiery wheels down slopes and throwing wooden disks into the air.[6] In the mystic Kabbalah of Judaism there are circles, the wheels of the heavens. When Buddha gave his first sermon it's said that he set in motion the wheel of the Dharma, symbolizing the endless spreading of Buddha's teachings. The ancient Hindu chakra system speaks of turning wheels of energy within our bodies. All of these are diverse expressions of the same awareness, one that unites the human family, and beyond.[7]

Not only is the circle an important component of spiritual

practice, it's also a practical blueprint. We humans are the ultimate toolmakers, and the natural world is the source of our inspiration. So it is that the circle is the blueprint for many of our own practical inventions. In fact, we seem to have an excellent grasp of the circle's properties, and we call upon them when we create our inventions. For example, a particularly practical early application was the earthenware pot. "A round pot…uses the minimum possible amount (and weight) of material to enclose a given volume…(so) we are assured that we've maximized the fraction of our effort that goes into carrying the water itself rather than its container."[8] The circle is also good blueprint for protection. Many cultures built dwellings in the shapes of cylinders and hemispheres, such as yurts, igloos, and tipis. Many war shields were also round, and when early pioneers were in danger they instinctively "circled the wagons".

Circles are vital to communication. The circle is found at the origin of almost all the alphabets or ideograms; they are common in the writings of many prehistoric and ancient peoples in many locations including the Orient, Europe, the Americas, and the Canary Islands.[9] This recognition of the role of the circle in facilitating communication is seen today: our modern communication equipment, such as satellites, satellite dishes, and radar dishes, are all circular. Circles enhance resonance, so we use them in designing many musical instruments such as drums, cymbals, clarinets, and oboes. The circle is also the blueprint for large containers where people gather, such as arenas and coliseums and many musical venues. Amphitheaters match the shape of sound waves and provide everyone with an equal view and sound experience.

Circular shapes can help us with focus and direction. The Circle is the basis for lenses in telescopes, microscopes, and glasses. We have used it to make instruments like the astrolabe, the sextant, and the gyroscope.

Circles have an inherent ability to present and facilitate relationship, which helps keep human beings oriented. An example is the compass. Circular in nature, it helps us with direction and with our relationship to the space that surrounds us. That orientation is based on the cycle created by the rising and setting of the sun and the cycles of the moon and the seasons. Circular sundials and clock faces are physical representations of the daily cycles that have given rise to the concept of "time," and its passage. These tools help us stay oriented to our life. The circle's facility with relationship can also be seen in the way gears, which are circular; engage each other to the benefit of a larger working order such as a watch or machine.

The circle's connection with movement is obvious. It provided the blueprint for the wheel, and for many other transportation technologies such as the propeller, the jet engine, and the turbine. We use round pistons in our engines because they make for better movement in the combustion process. Ballistics also relies on circles; round cylinders ensure the speed of bullets.

Perhaps most salient to our discussion is the circle's role in early commerce. Money began as a symbol, a placeholder. In the beginning, trade was intended to be an exchange of equal value. In short, it was a circle. On occasion, however, an exchange could not be completed, perhaps because a crop had not yet been harvested, or a basket not yet woven, or because one individual did not want or need what the other had to offer in exchange at the time. Then, money was used to hold a place in the cycle until the trade could be fulfilled, and the circle completed. The intention was always to keep things in motion, so the earliest forms of money—beads, shells, and coins—were symbolically round; they were meant to signify that the flow of exchange was ongoing, and would flow to completion. Originally, money was circular because it was meant to move. The rectangular shape of today's currency is indicative of our trying to hold onto, even hoard, something that was originally meant to flow.

By journeying through these myriad examples, we see that humanity has had a long relationship with the Circle. We also begin to see a great commonality. The Circle unites us across cultures, and through the ages. It inspires our creativity on the earthly plane, and connects us to the sacred dimension. We humans have had a long, multi-dimensional relationship with the circle. But how and why did the circle become such an important force in human consciousness?

Origins: The World is Round

The Circle is much more than a mere shape, or a symbol; it actually encompasses a deep philosophical understanding of the essential nature of the universe, as accrued by human beings through their direct experience over eons.

The Circle's significance comes from this simple truth: The Circle is the most important pattern of the cosmos. From our first moments as an embryo enclosed in the roundness of the womb, the Circle exerts its influence. The universe and everything in it begins with the Circle. Just think of how many circles there are in the natural world. They are everywhere in existence. We live on planet Earth, which is a sphere in movement: a multi-dimensional circle. The moon circles the Earth, the Earth circles the Sun. Our entire solar system consists of orbs—planets and moons—circulating in ellipses around other orbs in awesome and majestic synchronization. And beyond our solar system, the Milky Way is made up of fiery spheres, stars, moving in a spiral. Beyond that, there are galaxies upon galaxies replete with shining orbs, all dancing as one to the "music of the spheres." With amazing and inexplicable order, these multi-dimensional circles breathe movement, energy, life itself, into the universe.

As the circles move in the heavens, so moves the force and power of the world. Whirlpools, hurricanes, tornadoes, volcanoes are all swirling spirals of water, wind, or fire—and energy. Cyclical processes such as photosynthesis and evaporation/condensation pervade nature. Seeds—many round to facilitate movement—scatter to the ground, sprout and grow into plants, come to fruition, die, and re-seed, continuing the circle of life. The motion of water smoothes stones into rounded shapes. From birds' nests to rainbows, nature shows her cards: she is a lover of circles, singing them forth in countless colors and substances.

Not only are circles all around us, they are also within our own bodies: our eyes and heads, breasts, bellies, and mouths are round. So are eggs and embryos. Many cells are round. Circular platelets course through our blood. Our veins are round in order to facilitate smoothest flow. So is the womb, which also undergoes a cyclic process, mirroring the waxing and waning found in nature.

Nature moves in circles. Life itself is a circle. A day, a year, the life of a plant or an animal, a human life—all these follow a circular pattern. Like daybreak, and a seed in spring, we emerge from the darkness into light. Like mid-day, the summer, a plant, we develop, grow, and bloom into the fullness of our being. Like sunset, the autumn, the crops planted in a field, we adapt, change, and mature. Like midnight, the winter, a field gone fallow, we age and eventually we die. Then it all merges again with the earth and the larger cycle of existence. And, in due time, the earth gives rise to new forms. The design of life is like the rings in a tree, or the layers of an onion: concentric cycles moving individually, yet in harmonic confluence. In fact, the Circle is the most ubiquitous shape or pattern found in nature. It is found all around us and within us; the universe is replete with orbs, cycles and spheres. In short, the Circle is where we all came from. And through the Circle we began to understand that all things are related, for it unifies us all.

Those of us who live in an industrial society have become inured to this striking and beautiful truth, but indigenous people who lived in close relationship to the land—our ancestors—long ago recognized that the Circle was great power.

To early humans the sky must have felt like an overturned bowl, the rounded theater of the primary circles of life: the sun and moon. This shaped our experience at the most basic level. In the words of Láné Saán Moonwalker, "They saw these orbs turning around them in the sky. They saw the sun and the moon were basically circular. They deduced that the earth was also probably circular, because when you turn, nothing is further away than anything else. Some of them realized it was a sphere."

These circles were the bringers of each new day, year and season. They ushered in alternating periods of light and dark, hosting the cyclical nature of life itself. Life would not exist but for these circles; and so our first relationship with the Circle was deep and primary, building from awe to reverence. The Circle unified all of existence, and sang of a majestic coherence that lies hidden within the loose threads of the world. This understanding is perhaps best expressed in the famous words of the great Lakota Sioux chief and visionary holy man, Black Elk:

"Everything the Power of the World does is done in circle. The sky is round, and I have heard that the earth is round like a ball, and so are all the stars. The wind, in its greatest power, whirls. Birds make their nests in circles, for theirs is the same religion as ours. The sun comes forth and goes down again in a circle. The moon does the same, and both are round. Even the seasons form a great circle in their changing, and always come back again to where they were. The life of a man is a circle from childhood to childhood, and so it is in everything where power moves."[10]

--Black Elk (1863-1950)

If everything in the universe happens in cycles, what does that mean for our human existence? This is the question that guided our ancestors. The answer to that question was simple: Humans, too, must live in circles. And so, for millennia, the Circle was the primary blueprint that human beings used to organize their lives. It was the principle organizing tool for most, if not all, ancient peoples: the aboriginals of Australia, South American Indians, the original Tibetans, Siberian people, African people, East Indian people, Oriental people. It was heavily used by the Celts in Britain long before Romans came, and in early North America as well.

Through Circles we humans have sought—and found—communion with the natural order. We have used it to create sacred space in which to center ourselves, and to seek guidance. And what is sacredness, but the recognition of the essential wholeness, unity, and oneness of the universe? We have almost lost this understanding, but it's still present in our language. The word "whole" is the same as the root of the word "holy," which is synonymous with "sacred." The whole is sacred.

The Circle became a reminder of that fundamental understanding. It became a very important element in the traditions of most, if not all, indigenous cultures across the globe. It became a sacred tool. Our ancestors used it to continuously remind themselves of the sacredness of existence, of the interrelatedness of everything, and to commune with the larger whole. They wove it into their basketry and incorporated it into their ceremonies, into their dances and rituals. Throughout the world, the Circle was used as a means to help us live in a harmonious relationship with each other, and the natural world. To keep the reminder ever-present, the Circle became the blueprint for many types of traditional housing. Polynesians constructed round structures; indigenous Mongolians built yurts, and the Inuit igloos. In North America, hogans, wigwams, and tipis were all based on the Circle. All believed that the circular design bestowed sacredness upon these earthly dwellings.[11] In constructing such homes they incorporated the sacred into everyday life. It served as a constant reminder, lest they forget.

"Humans do forget," says Láné Saán Moonwalker. "We continuously forget our true place in the natural order. It's our nature to get out of balance and harmony. We'll tend to get insecure, and put ourselves first. These early people knew this. They lived too close together not to have that understanding. They knew that they needed reminders, and the Circle became their reminder. The Circle is still there to remind all of us to move back into the space of humility, respect, and harmonization with what is."

Implicit in the universality of the Circle was an acknowledgement and nonjudgmental acceptance of human frailty. The reality of human existence is that we must live in two realms: the material and the non-material. These are both aspects of our being, and that reality presents us with major challenges. How do we negotiate the non-material realm, balancing its callings with material demands and concerns? How do we deal with those things that we cannot see, taste, smell, touch, or measure?

As humans, we have a tendency to fragment and get out of balance. It's in our nature. The Circle, however, presented the wholeness of all. It showed how the power of the world moves, from the dark to the light, and back again, from the non-material realm into the material realm, and returning. In this way, the spirit and the body were not split apart, as they are in modern day, but unified in wholeness. In this way, the connection between the sacred and the practical was never lost—as it has been in Western cultures.

Like humans, a tree has its roots in the earth and reaches toward the sky. But, unlike humans, the tree successfully unites the two realms, and reminds us to do the same. Trees carry this powerful message for us; they remind us that balance is possible. This is why trees are so important to the cosmologies of many indigenous peoples: the tree is a teacher and a bridge between the two realms of material and non-material. The center of the Circle houses this "sacred tree" concept.

Throughout time, we humans have used the Circle as a tool for gaining wisdom about how to live. We have used it to set ourselves in proper relationship with the rest of creation, and to align ourselves with the energies flowing through the universe. We have used it to gain insight and direction on very practical matters. We have sat in council circles. We have used it to give us wheels, so that we might move as the heavens did. Through the ages, many strove to learn from and live in harmony with all that the Circle represents. This is not to say that the lives of these early people were perfect—far from it. These were imperfect, emergent humans who, no doubt, constantly fell out of balance and grace. But beneath the human disorder and befuddlement there was a powerful tool: the Circle.

In this way, the Circle came to be more than a geometric shape. It became the sacred expression of this understanding of the nature of existence. It served as a perpetual reminder to humans of the essential circular nature of life with its innate interdependence, interconnections, and concentricity. It became the container for the accumulated wisdom of the experiences of humans about how to live. The Circle was venerated and respected. It was the touchstone by which we measured our humanity.

The Gifts of the Circle: How the Circle Can Help Us

The central premise of this book is that the Circle can be of tremendous help and support to us in business and in life.

To our ancestors, something so universal as the Circle held vast power. Anything so pervasive must be worthy of contemplation and study. So, some endeavored to learn all they could about the Circle. Over time, some began to understand that the Circle is an amazingly robust blueprint, with myriad strengths and few limitations. This makes the Circle an extremely powerful ally and tool for humans.

We have lost touch with much of what we once understood about the Circle. We have forgotten about what an important resource it really is. But, fortunately, that ancient knowledge of the Circle has not vanished forever. It has been kept alive and nurtured. It's now offered to all who are willing to listen, so that we might consider bringing its gifts into businesses, to the greater benefit of all.

The Circle's Gifts: What the Circle Can Help Us Do

- Create and maintain good Relationships
- Generate Movement
- Get in touch with what is True
- Create and Maintain Boundaries
- Attain Clarity
- Maintain Neutrality
- Focus our Attention
- Hold an Altruistic Agenda
- Gain Sense of Direction
- Bridge and Translate between entities
- Practice Moderation and Balance
- Practice Humility
- Embrace Sharing
- Practice Equitable Exchange
- Create effective Structures
- Learn from the Past
- Grow & Evolve Our Business (and ourselves)
- Find Unity in Diversity
- Consider More of the Whole
- Connect with the Sacred

As we've said, each of the universal blueprints has innate

characteristics. The better we understand these characteristics, the better equipped we will be to choose the blueprint that's most appropriate for what we want to accomplish. To take full advantage of this amazingly robust tool we, too, must learn about these gifts of the Circle. So, let us begin. Because of its essential nature, the Circle has the innate power to help us:

• Create and Maintain Good Relationships –

Businesses are built on relationships: they are fundamental to business's existence. Yet, we are relatively unskilled in how to create relationships that really work, *i.e.,* relationships that are healthy, equitable, mutually beneficial, and sustainable.

In business, the key to good relationships is to consciously set up structures and patterns that encourage mutually beneficial exchanges. Because the Circle is present in everything from cells to stars, the Circle can relate to everything and everyone. It has the innate ability to include everyone and to take virtually anything into consideration. Because the Circle is naturally attuned to relationship, it's the best blueprint to use when we want to create good ones. In short, a good relationship is a Circle. We will learn more about how later in this volume, and in Volume 2.

• Generate Movement –

Every business needs momentum; forward movement is what keeps a business alive. Some structures facilitate movement better than others. The workings of the solar system with its perpetually moving spheres and ellipses show us clearly that the Circle is the shape of continuous movement.

A circular structure is much more able to sustain momentum than a linear structure. The Circle has no beginning and no end. Once an impulse of movement is introduced into a circle, it's *always there*, cycling around and around. Energy does not deteriorate as it does in linear structures; it's self-renewing. By basing your business on the Circle blueprint, you will enhance the flow of energy in the business. This includes the flow of thought and production, the flow of personnel and management, as well as the flow of finances. People's energy will be invigorated. As a result, the organization is never static. You will have enhanced the likelihood of success.

- **Get in Touch with What is True –**

As we've said, the exclusive use of linear thinking makes us vulnerable to illusion. This happens because when we are proceeding on a linear trajectory, our vision gets narrow. We get emotionally invested in getting to the goal. That further restricts our vision. From this point forward, we tend to believe what we want to believe is true. This can be very costly, as we can invest too much or too long in products or projects that are not really viable. To be successful in business, we need to be in touch with the truth.

Besides having the intrinsic properties of relationship and movement, the Circle also has an innate connection with what is real and true from a universal, non-human-centric perspective. Because the Circle is not a human invention, it's not subject to our biases or prejudices. It's aligned with something greater, the flow of Universal Energy, as we will explain in a subsequent chapter. When we work with the Circle we are more open to the "universal truth" of what is. This helps free us from illusion so that we don't waste time or energy.

These three qualities—relationship, movement, and the ability to connect us with universal truth—convey the most essential essence of the Circle. Whenever we engage with the Circle, these qualities are always present, first and foremost. Beyond these, the Circle has many more attributes that make it an extremely practical tool for business.

• Create and Maintain Boundaries –

The ability to delineate boundaries is very important in both life and in business. Boundaries are important because *they give us our identity*. A clear boundary helps us define what's "us" and what's "not us." It tells us that there is one kind of energy on the inside of the boundary, and another kind of energy on the outside. If there is no clear, set boundary, then there is no individual identity. This is true for a business, just as it is for a human being. In the business world the question of boundaries shows up in span of control issues, in questions about who has ownership of what, in turf battles, and in the definition of policies and procedures.

Generally speaking, we have a poor comprehension of boundaries. Consequently, have a hard time respecting boundaries in practice. We trample over the boundaries of others incessantly, and even tend toward consumptive behavior with respect to our own boundaries. The Circle is actually defined by its discrete boundary, whereas the line is not. This gives the Circle a much more profound knowledge of boundaries, and therefore we can use it to help us to create and maintain good boundaries.

• Attain Clarity –

Many times in our life experience we feel confused about what we want or what we should do. This is because we are bombarded with agendas from many sources: friends, relatives, the media, advertising agencies, our culture, the government, religion, employers and employees, etc., etc. This creates a great deal of static that we must sort through. The Circle can help.

When we work with the Circle, its distinct boundary creates a clear space within which to work. Because the energy of the Circle is not human, the inner space is free of human investments. This gives the space a special quality that we experience as acceptance and non-judgment. This is a space in which we can consider options without the static created by human judgment, righteousness, or doubt impinging on our process. Without the confusion of human emotions and projections clouding our view, we see issues more clearly; potential stumbling blocks are more apparent.

• Maintain Neutrality–

Many times, important decisions require leaders to be able to maintain neutrality until all the necessary input has been received. As a wheel moves, the rims turn, but the hub is still. This is how the Circle functions. Energy is in constant movement on the perimeter, while within the Circle there is stillness. In this way the Circle creates a neutral space where we can gain perspective, while still being connected to the flow of movement that is intrinsic to life. This stillness allows and enables us to better witness and to accept *what is* without judgment or fear. The Circle enables us to remain connected to the flow of movement and productivity outside the Circle—yet not be overrun by it. This allows us to have better orientation, direction, and focus.

• Attain Focus –

The business world is becoming so complex that it's often difficult to stay focused. The circular shape is innately linked to focus because, by its very nature, the circle creates a boundary around an area (*i.e.,* an energetic field), separating it from everything else outside. The roundness of that boundary brings our attention to the center. (There are no distracting corners.) This naturally helps us to focus on what is within the boundary.

• Hold an Altruistic Agenda –

All of our actions—in business and in life—should be guided by altruism, which means to do *that which is best for all concerned, including oneself.* This is an extremely important concept. It is often misunderstood and misinterpreted.

The Circle's boundary creates a very special kind of space: sacred space. The nature of that space helps us to take a more holistic perspective, and to consider what is best for all concerned, including ourselves. We will discuss altruism at length later in this volume.

- **Orient to our Environment & Find Direction –**

As we've said, the linear pattern cannot orient us or give us a good sense of direction, though this is something that people crave. Human beings become oriented through a sense of relationship. As we discussed previously, relationship is a fundamental quality of the Circle. We can see this in the way a compass, circular in nature, helps us orient to the space that surrounds us. A circular watch or sundial helps us orient to the passage of time. In addition, the Circle's essential affinity with movement means that it can give us a sense of direction by showing us the path of the flow.

- **Bridge and Translate –**

Communication is central to business. Creating connections between entities that may not have much knowledge of each other, whether they be suppliers, contract employees, or project team members, is essential. When different entities come together, they each bring their unique energy. Sometimes this creates problems of translation. Because the Circle is found in everything, it has great commonality with everything. Thus, the Circle has the innate capacity to facilitate the translation of all the different kinds of input provided by all the different individuals involved.

In the realm of aerodynamics we know that rounder shapes facilitate the smooth movement of machines through the air. That is why the wing and nose of a plane are rounded. Automobiles are also designed with many curved surfaces, because they minimize resistance. So, too, if we what to build bridges between people, to facilitate the flow of communication between them, and to minimize resistance to each other's input, we'll want to use the Circle as the blueprint.

• Practice Moderation and Balance –

As we've said, human beings have a tendency to go to extremes. This is in our nature, but frequently it doesn't serve us. In business, this tendency often leads us into behavior that is at odds with our ethics. The ability to practice balance and moderation is very important, as these are the keys to being supported by the flow of Universal Energy, as we will explain in a later chapter.

The Circle's very structure speaks to us of moderation and balance: Every point on the Circle is equidistant from the center. There is no extreme in the Circle. So, the Circle can help us contain our extremism. It constantly reminds us, and guides us in the direction of moderation.

• Embrace Sharing –

In business and in life, we need a sense of completion and closure. It's often missing in our culture, because we do not understand what brings it about. A sense of fulfillment and completion comes from giving back. We complete the cycle when we share the fruits of labor, when we share our abundance (in the form of goods, wealth, or knowledge) with all those who have contributed to creating it.

Because we experience true completion so rarely, we long for it without knowing exactly what we are craving. The Circle can help us to embrace sharing as a natural part of our process. It can teach us how to share in a balanced way, avoiding the extremes of stinginess or self-sacrifice.

- **Practice Equitable Exchange** –

The conduct of business involves multiple transactions. These transactions work best, and are most rewarding and satisfying, when they are equitable and mutually beneficial. Today, many are not. Too many times we seek to turn things to solely to our own advantage. Perhaps we have assumed that it cannot be otherwise. This is not so. We can learn from the Circle how to turn our human transactions into equitable exchanges.

All natural processes are *cycles* in which there is a process of mutually beneficial exchange, of receiving and giving back. We enter into this great process of exchange when we draw our first breath. We breathe in oxygen and breathe out carbon dioxide, thus helping support plant life. The breath of life is a part of a greater Circle. The universe is *always in the process of creating balance and harmony*. The process by which it creates this balance is *equitable exchange*. We have the opportunity to participate in this universal process of balance and harmony with every transaction. The Circle can show us how.

- **Practice Humility** -

Humility would seem to have little relevance for the world of business. However, when we operate out of our egocentrism we create imbalance and disharmony. Ultimately, this does not benefit us. It's much more rational for us to recognize and acknowledge, for example, the degree to which we are dependent upon others— our customers, suppliers, fellow employees, the community, and the Earth itself—for our business to succeed.

The practice of humility creates greater balance and harmony. The Circle vision states that if one studies the underlying design of the universe, one sees that no being or species is preferred. All are equally important and valuable; nothing is greater or lesser than anything else. If humans are to live harmoniously with the nature of existence, we must acknowledge and live in accordance with this fundamental truth. This requires us to practice true humility, which is a challenge for humans. The rewards are great, however: we live a much more harmonious life. Because the Circle is equal in all directions, this blueprint can call help us create equitable structures and processes where we can learn to practice humility. That's why we call upon the Circle whenever we want to create a democratic forum where everyone has an equal voice.

- **Create Effective Structures -**

The question of structure permeates business life. In fact, corporate management is so convinced that structure is imperative that restructuring is seen as one of the most viable options for rectifying business problems. Questions about structure arise all the time in business. Here are some typical examples:

- How should my business, department, or team be structured?
- Will a new or different structure actually bring about the results we want?

We submit that most of us do not really grasp the essentials of structure. Many of the decisions we make about it are only partly informed. The circle *is* a structure, so it understands the nature of structure. This intimate knowledge means that we can turn to the Circle to learn about the nature of structure. Furthermore, we can use the Circle as a blueprint to create effective structures and processes for our businesses.

Most of the structures and processes we use now are based on a linear pattern. Most business processes are linear: they take us from point A to point B. Most business organizations are hierarchical, which is based on the triangle blueprint. These structures have very definite limitations and vulnerabilities, as we will discuss in more detail in Volume 2. Meantime, we have forgotten the power of circular structures and processes. Circular structures are very efficient. They facilitate equitability; they sustain momentum while being self-renewing, and conserve energy. They support growth and evolution. Human beings function very well within circular structures and processes because they feel very natural to us.

• Learn from the Past –

Would we be more effective, if we regularly evaluated the effects of our actions? Surely there are lessons to be learned from past actions that can be applied to the present and future. The line just takes us forward, without a sense of where we've been, and only a limited sense of where we're going. When we are driven by the linear pattern, we often forget to stop and evaluate our progress. If we do engage with evaluation, the process is quite often truncated. We can easily slip into trying to vindicate our actions, rather than trying to learn from our mistakes. Our linear trajectory does not provide any structural support for reviewing the past and refining our thinking based on what we can learn from it. From grade school on up, we learn to be afraid of losing our place in line, so we don't want to go back. Unless there is a real and specific push to do so, everything we've done in the past remains in the past. We just keep going forward, often repeating the same mistakes.

When you use the Circle as your primary blueprint, however, you quite literally "come around again." This repetition of cycles means your process is always getting refined, in a continuous manner. You're learning from your mistakes as you come back around, and truly evaluating what you have been doing. This is built into the Circle process.

The Circle also creates an energetic environment where reflection and learning are possible. As we have said, the Circle is truly universal because it exists in everything, from cells to stars. It is supportive of everything that exists, without judgment. This imbues the Circle with a special quality that we experience as acceptance and non-judgment. When we work with this type of energy, we feel safe enough to open to new information. We are free to learn, rather than clinging to what we think we know, or needing to be right. This enables us to look and name the truth of things with much less apprehension.

- **Grow & Evolve** –

In order for any business to stay alive, it must grow and evolve. By "grow" we do not mean just get bigger, but actually develop and mature.

In linear structures, we often experience change as a struggle. This is because we're fighting *against* the structure. Linear structures do not have the flexibility to adapt easily. As we've said, the Circle holds within it the essential implication of the repetition of cycles. As the circle repeats, it never stays the same; it lifts to a spiral. The spiral is the very pattern of evolutionary growth. It's in the double helix of DNA, as well as the Golden Mean. The Circle, therefore, has an intimate knowledge of, and inherently supports, the ongoing process of growth and evolution. When we employ circular structures and processes, evolutionary change and adaptation will flow much more naturally. Maturity is intrinsic to this process.

- **Find the Unity in Diversity, and Vice-Versa** -

When we operate out of linearity, we tend to see the world as made up of opposing forces, and mutually exclusive options. By definition, this is stressful and conflict inducing. This is because of the nature of the line: it originated as the connection of two points. It never brings those two points together in any kind of unity; it only moves from one to the other.

In contrast, the Circle is inherently unifying: it can help bring us together. It exists in and/or about everything that exists; there is not anything that does not interact with or relate to the Circle in some way. The Circle is the quintessential "networker". As we shall see in later chapters, the Circle embodies a process that enables us to work effectively with multiple aspects of a situation as a whole.

There is often a lot of fragmentation in businesses. Groups contend with each other for resources, or have conflicting priorities. Humans have a tendency to reject input they don't agree with or relate to, but the Circle process provides a model of acceptance. In this way, it helps facilitate holistic thinking by acknowledging and respecting all input as part of the whole. Circular structures and processes can enable both management and workers to see, understand, and work more effectively with the business as a whole. We'll learn more about the Circle process in a later chapter.

• Consider More of the Whole -

Reductionism told us that we could understand the whole by breaking it down into its component parts and analyzing them. In so doing, we lost sight of the whole.

Because the Circle can relate to anything that exists, it has the ability to bridge to anything, anywhere, anytime, any place. Its essential wholeness can encompass and transcend all the complementary aspects of life that we now see as dualities: the physical and the spiritual, the practical and the sacred, thinking and feeling, masculine and feminine, yin and yang. Therefore, if we use the Circle as our underlying blueprint, we'll be able to work with more aspects of any situation, issue, or problem. We do not have to feel fragmented. Working with the Circle moves us out of the reductionistic thinking that has colored much of Western experience.

• Connect with the Sacred -

The use of the Circle as a sacred space is ancient. Circles were used as a means to help individual human beings heal and gain a greater sense of clarity about a challenge they or their group were facing.

~ Business Revolution through Ancestral Wisdom ~

To gain greater individual clarity, a person would go and sit within a circle that he or she had created using natural objects such as stones, shells, or bones. They would orient the Circle to the four directions. The process was done in a very deliberate way, as a kind of preparatory meditation. They would humbly ask the different directions if they would be willing to work with them on their question or issue. Before actually entering the Circle, they would perform a ceremonial cleansing, perhaps by burning sage or another herb, and moving the smoke over their body with their hands (called smudging). This helped to clear them from attachments. The intention was to enter the sacred space with a heart, mind and spirit that were purified, and as open as possible to receiving wisdom.

They entered the Circle in order to seek guidance. By creating a physical circle, they created a space that was sacred. It honored the most basic blueprint for all of creation. The boundary around that space delineated a space where human wants and agendas did not intrude. This space was to be a vessel where one could commune with the wisdom of the ancestors through a pure channel. If one approached the Circle appropriately, with adequate respect and true humility, one would be gifted with a concrete experience of the wholeness of existence. If one emptied one's self of selfish concerns, one could feel and perceive the inter-relatedness of all things. And, through this experience, one's path, one's part in the co-creation of the future, would become clearer. One could realize how to act for the benefit of all concerned, including one's self. One could see how to support the co-evolution of their people and the earth. The Circle was a portal to wisdom.

This use of the Circle is the most important for us to understand. These indigenous people implicitly understood that this process of clarification required them to traverse between multiple dimensions in order to come to a higher level of understanding, balance, and unity. They knew they needed to bridge their personal process with the larger, spiritual process, weaving the two together. They knew they needed to connect their mundane life with the energetic flow of existence so that the two were in harmony. They knew the Circle is an inherently holistic tool—a sacred container—that is uniquely capable of holding the continuity of all of those dimensions.

It's important for us to appreciate this, because our culture lacks such a tool. Because we lack a way of grasping wholeness, we fear being overwhelmed. And so, rather than dealing with the wholeness of life, we lean on reductionism. We take wholeness apart, so that we can deal with only one aspect of it. The trade-off is that we tend to lose our sense of the Whole, and we become fragmented. We think in terms of oppositions and dichotomies rather than seeing differences as different aspects of the whole.

The difference is profound. Native people felt—and many still feel—a deep connection with all of existence. They felt embedded within the web of the universe, and held a profound reverence for it. Furthermore, they found a way to maintain a connection with that wholeness so that they could turn to it for guidance.

Through its very being, the Circle offers us the opportunity to connect with and actually have a concrete experience of sacred space—a space that is beyond human agendas, a space that is a portal to wisdom. We, too, can use the Circle to create sacred space.

The Death of the Circle

Once, we humans understood the power of the Circle. In time, however, the human population came across situations that seemed to require another pattern. If a group of people needed to be mobilized and moved quickly to avoid a disaster, the Circle wouldn't do. There was no time for anything holistic or complex. The need was to move from point A to point B, now! This is exactly what the linear pattern helps us do.

These frequent speedy migrations—often sparked by fear of impending doom—reinforced the line as a useful, even life-saving, pattern. Somewhere "along the line," whether because of necessity, sloth, fear, or zeal, we got hooked, and the line began to become the dominant pattern. We even began to believe the line to be a whole blueprint. But the line didn't completely supplant the Circle until we came to the Industrial Revolution. This kicked linearity into high gear. We decided that the best way to organize for mass production was a production line. Under the industrial model, the average worker was not supposed to be thinking about the whole process, just their little part of it. Those in positions of authority were charged with figuring out whole. The importance of considering the wholeness of a situation or issue was significantly diminished. Perhaps the best example of this linear perspective can be found in the way the railroads were built in the United States. The imperative was to get from one coast to another without much attention to working on a sense of cohesiveness within the country. This encapsulates the linear approach to going about things, which persists—and dominates—to this day.

This enormous, wrenching, and revolutionary change had a significant impact on our consciousness. As the linear trajectory picked up speed, the earth became a storehouse of raw materials to be harvested, processed, and turned into consumable products. Land was to be developed. More and more energy was required to keep the line going. Human beings became commodities. Today, we are not so much citizens to be consulted, but consumers to be wooed. We are "human resources" that can be consumed and discarded. Indigenous cultures and other species are disappearing at an alarming rate (scientific consensus says we are currently in the throes of a mass extinction).[12] As a consequence of this ever-increasing linear trajectory our eco-systems are over-burdened, and the human species appears unsustainable.

For all intents and purposes, the Circle, with all its inherent power and meaning, including its profound ability to keep us connected to the natural world of which we are a part, disappeared. As a way of life, it virtually vanished from the face of the Earth. It faded from our consciousness. We threw it away, and even some indigenous people began to forget.

We have lost touch with much of what we once understood about the Circle. We have forgotten about what an important resource it really is. In throwing away the Circle, we threw away one of the most precious gifts that has ever been presented to us.

~ Business Revolution through Ancestral Wisdom ~

Fortunately, the Circle is not lost. It's not lost because some indigenous people did not forget. They have carried this wisdom, and kept it alive until such time as we would again discover that we needed it. They have kept it alive, and are now offering it to all who are willing to listen. It's not lost because the Circle lives within each of us. It's part of us, and we are part of it. It's waiting to be rediscovered and brought to life again in the modern world. It's waiting to once again be used as an agent of profound connection, as a sacred tool, and as a teacher of the human spirit. It's waiting for our request for its help.

These, then, are some of the gifts the Circle blueprint can bring into the realm of modern business. The Circle is also the best tool we have for working with our most important business resource: energy. We turn to that topic next.

Chapter Three
Working with Energy

We're all familiar with "energy" as a term describing the power we derive from burning fossil fuels or harnessing sunlight, but there are many more forms of energy that are important to business. In fact, everything we do in business involves some type of energy. Energy is necessary for movement, focus, motivation, and manifestation, all of which are fundamental to the conduct of business. You might even say that the conduct of business is, in many ways, synonymous with the *management of energy*. Energy, then, is a potentially powerful resource for any business. But how well do we know how to work with it? What if we could get better at reading and working with energy? Wouldn't that be a boon to any business?

Fortunately, we have an innate ability to sense energy. We're always responding to different kinds of energy; we simply don't realize it. When we get a feeling that a new product just is (or isn't) right, or that the timing of a deal is (or isn't) good, we're sensing energy. We're tuning into energetic flows. We may tend to minimize or rationalize these perceptions, but many of the people who are most successful in business actually work very effectively with energy—they're just not aware of it.

The ability to read and manage energy is a distinct advantage in business. The Circle can be a tremendous help in the management of energy, but before we discuss this, let's explore a little more about how energy relates to business.

Energy Basics

Energy is all about movement. And, because everything in the universe is made up of energy, everything in the universe is always in movement. That movement may not be perceptible to us humans, but it's ongoing and continuous. It is an endlessly flowing river. Everything is always in flow; everything is always in the process of changing and evolving.

Energy always wants to flow; that is its nature. Energies are in a constant state of movement; energy fields interact with each other in dynamic ways, like weather fronts. One supports the other, one leads to the other, and so on. This interaction of energies creates a continuous flow that is always available for us to interact with—and draw support from.

Sometimes, however, we humans create roadblocks that inhibit the flow of energy, leading to adverse consequences for others and ourselves. One of the reasons we do this is because, being innately insecure, we want to hold on to things. We fear change, and so we want to keep things as they are, lest we get swept away by that timeless river. The irony is that we're actually changing all the time; our own physical being is always in a process of renewal. We fall out of touch with this truth and so we get out of touch with the nature of the universe. If we become more conscious of the true nature of reality, we'll be less likely to do things that block the flow. The more conscious we become, the more we'll be able to make use of energy as the powerful business resource that it is.

The ability to recognize blocked energy is a distinct business advantage. Here's why: When energy is blocked from flowing it shows up as unmet needs or unsolved problems and dilemmas. These unmet needs and unsolved problems are really business opportunities looking for solutions.

When energy is blocked, it creates a certain kind of pattern on the physical plane. That's how you can recognize it. A traffic jam is an obvious example. In business you might see evidence of energy blockages in the unsatisfactory flow of paperwork or order fulfillment. A rise in customer complaints or a downturn in accounts receivable can also signify that the flow of energy is being blocked in some way. Here is another aspect of energy flow that should really help us in business. Whenever the flow of energy is blocked, that blocked energy begins to pool. As the energy pools, it builds. That gathering pool of energy becomes a reservoir of creative potential. This means that *for every instance of blocked energy, there is an accompanying build-up of energetic support for any endeavor that will successfully unblock that energy and set it flowing again.*

Energetically speaking, then, every unmet need or problem also holds within it the potential for its solution. The bigger the blockage, the greater the energetic support for a solution. Looking at the world through this lens can give us a rejuvenating perspective on major social problems. In the United States, for example, there are many needs crying out to be addressed. They include the need to:

- Recover integrity in the realm of politics
- Restructure healthcare
- Conserve and restore natural resources
- Conduct business in a more socially responsible and beneficial way
- Create more opportunities for economic well-being
- Create a culture that is more supportive of our children's development

These problems can seem overwhelming. If we look at them through the lens of energy, however, we can see that these same social problems are also indications of the build-up of a tremendous amount of potential creative energy that we can use to solve them. We can see that these needs represent extraordinary opportunities for people with motivation and creativity to come up with well thought-out approaches for meeting those needs. Their efforts will have a tremendous amount of momentum behind them.

In sum, then, blocked energy signals opportunity. These opportunities show up as unmet needs and unresolved problems. To our interest, humans are exceptionally gifted at creative problem-solving. When we come up with solutions (in the form of ideas, inventions, innovations, tools and methods) that truly address the causes of the blockages, that blocked energy is released and is able to flow again. Such solutions and their creators will receive a great deal of support from the Universe because they are helping facilitate the ongoing flow of energy. From an energetic perspective, then, a *business is an agent of energy flow*. Conversely, any business that does not support the ongoing flow of energy, or blocks the flow of energy in some way, will have a harder time being successful over the long-term.

When we discover blocked energy, the next step is to analyze and "parse" the blockage to determine what type of energy is being blocked. This is key to creating effective solutions. For example, in the case of our health care system, what is the primary type of energy that is being blocked? Is it economic? What is the root cause of that blockage? What kind of solution could truly free the blocked economic flow? Are there other types of energy blockages as well? Is that why the problem seems so unsolvable?

There are actually many different types of energy in the universe. Many of these come into play in business. Learning to read the energy dynamics that are in play in any particular situation gives us access to a deeper level of reality. As we become more acutely aware of these dynamics, we'll be better able to notice blockages in energetic flow, and to identify what type of energy is being blocked. Then we can develop solutions that help get the energy flowing again, to the advantage of our business and the greater Whole.

Types of Human Energy

There is another aspect to learning to work with energy.

Human beings operate on the basis of many different types of energy. Each of these energy types has its gifts. Each can be used in constructive or destructive ways—and each can be taken to extremes. Let's start by considering the types of energy that characterize human beings.

- **Personal Electro-Magnetic Energy —**

Known as our electro-magnetic (E-M) field, this energy is created by our metabolic process, and is a by-product of that process. We store the spill-off energy from this process in an energy field around us. This energy field is connected to our body, and it resides on the outside of our skin about 4-10 inches all around us. This is our own personal, intimate energy.

Each individual's energy field is unique. In general, this energy is very vibrant, focused, and normally very full-bodied, even aggressive. Its main purpose is to be a resource for us when we need extra energy, to help us recharge when we are tired and stressed, or to help us when we are sick by boosting our immune system. Our E-M field is also our natural biofeedback resource.

We can call upon our E-M field for extra energy when we're experiencing stress about a personal situation, such as a relationship, finances, or "the job." We need to be careful how we employ it, however, because we can use it to push people away, to argue or attack others verbally, or to act out our feelings towards others. If we use our E-M field too much in this way, we will not have any reserve left to help us when we really need it. Personal E-M energy is fragile and limited. It can be re-charged, but it's finite, just as we are. We need to manage it well.

How does personal energy relate to business? As a manager, you can use the conscious understanding of this energy to support the health and well-being of your personnel. You'll be able to help them recognize signs of stress and help them manage it. Your ability to assess another's personal E-M energy field is very important when considering the pacing of a task. Your ability to realistically assess and work with your employees' personal E-M energy supports productivity and customer satisfaction. All of this leads to more business.

• Kinetic Energy (Physical Energy)—

This is the energy we create whenever our physical bodies move in any way, no matter how small. We engage with this energy when we watch or play sports, watch movies, go dancing, eat together, engage in sexual activities, sing and play games together. Kinetic energy is personal and finite, making it vulnerable.

Obviously, this energy is important in many workplaces. We engage with this energy when we are working on a construction site, serving tables at a restaurant, making products on an assembly line, teaching in a classroom, or processing transactions at a bank. We can use this energy very constructively to help resolve many personnel issues, deal with production difficulties, and straighten out work safety problems.

Kinetic energy is often problematic, because it's attached to the body and is related to a wide gamut of areas that we may have issues with. This energy is involved in personal grooming habits, sexual habits, eating habits, sleeping habits, walking styles, sitting styles, and body language of all kinds. This energy also relates to our style of response to injury or other kinds of pain that is expressed through body movement. Others' kinetic energy can trigger our prejudices. We can get abusive in our attempts to manage this energy in others, such as placing unnecessary restrictions on others' personal movement or habits that make us uncomfortable.

• Emotional Energy—

As long as there are humans, there will be emotional energy. Because humans predominantly react to things from their emotions, we are constantly engaging with emotional energy.

Whenever we engage with our emotions, we contribute to a standing pool of emotional energy. Because we're wired for emotions, we're constantly feeding the pool of emotional energy around us. When we become emotional we can tap into this pool. Our emotions then become amplified, and they can even spread from person to person. This is why emotions feel "contagious."

Emotional energy is quite complex and powerful. We often find it overwhelming. Humans are actually rather immature emotionally, and we over-use our minds to compensate. Emotional energy is unpredictable, and when we take it to extremes it leads to unclear behavior and erratic thinking. We're very susceptible to emotional energy, whether it be our own, or that of others. Because of this, it's not uncommon to feel concern and even fear when we are around someone who is engaging recklessly with emotional energy. Here are a few key signs to help you recognize if you are in the presence of extreme emotional energy:

- Are you feeling suddenly very tired?
- Are you feeling very hungry, even though you have not done much physical work?
- Does volatility abound?
- Are silly and non-thinking mistakes common?
- Are you engulfed by feelings of desperation and lack?
- Do things feel like they're going to extremes all the time?
- Has trauma/drama become the norm?

As you might surmise, emotional energy is very much abused in this present time. When used in destructive ways, it fans the embers of hate. It becomes the basis for riots, domestic violence, and war. Emotional energy can be used constructively. Examples include inspiring others to get involved in a humanitarian or environmental project, exhorting others to help save a family in distress, or challenging us to rebuild our economy. But even the constructive use of emotional energy can be taken to an extreme, often in the workplace. We can get too emotionally invested in well-intentioned projects or products. This can lead to the over-consumption of energy, physical resources, even our health and well-being.

Because this energy is so complex and powerful, we must learn to deal with it very consciously. We tend to have a lot of judgments about emotions. That's because we don't really understand them very well. Emotions are just energetic shifts that evolved to help us survive. A basic understanding of emotions will be helpful.

The Five Basic Emotions & Their Purposes:

Human beings experience five basic emotions: fear, anger, grief, love, and joy. All of our more complex emotions are various combinations of these. Emotions are not just random reactions to events; each of these basic emotions has a unique and specific purpose. They are as follows:

- Fear is an energetic shift that helps us to respond to a threatening situation. The purpose of fear is to make us aware of something needing to be done.
- Anger is an emotion that tends to arise in response to a feeling of fear. Its purpose is to motivate us to do something in order to help ensure our survival.
- Grief is an emotional response that arises to help us let go of fear and anger. Its purpose is to help us become resolved about an unchangeable situation and get on with life. Grieving is extremely important to emotional well-being. Unless we release and let go of fear and anger, there is no room for the emotions of love and joy.
- Love is possible when fear, anger, and grief have been released. Its purpose is the nurturance of self and others.
- Joy arises out of love. The purpose of joy is to help us restore and re-charge.

When an emotion is used for its true purpose, there is always a positive outcome. It's the mis-use of an emotion, i.e., the use of an emotion for something other than its true purpose, that leads to problems. Let's take anger as an example. As we said, anger arises in response to a fear. The purpose of anger is to create an energetic shift within us, to motivate us to do something that will help us survive. If we find ourselves getting angry, and then take a moment to get in touch with the purpose of our anger, we can see that it is arising in order to move us out of danger. We can then choose to move in the direction of survival. If we respond accordingly, the energy of anger quickly dissipates because it's done its job. We then become emotionally clear and serene. That's using an emotion for its original purpose. If you observe a duck pond you can see this dynamic in action. When two ducks come upon the same breadcrumb there may be quick, angry flap of wings, but the moment passes quickly. When it's over, it's over. There is no residual anger. The surface of the pond becomes calm again, mirroring the serenity that ensues.

It's when we use our anger for something other than its true purpose that we get off track. For example, we might become angry when we are told that we neglected a duty. The true purpose of that anger is to motivate us to get out of a fearful situation. If we acknowledge our mistake and learn how to avoid it in the future, the matter is likely to be resolved quickly. If, however, we give into our anger and make excuses, try to shift our responsibilities to another, or try to blame them for our situation, that's a mis-use of the true purpose of the emotion. The situation does not clear, and residual anger remains.

Obviously, emotional energy affects the workplace environment. People bring this energy into the workplace, and it affects others. Management can take steps to regulate the flow of emotional energy. A dramatic event, such as a plant closing or a significant downsizing, for example, will trigger a lot of emotional energy. If this energy is not processed effectively, it will become blocked. Unless that blocked energy is freed, productivity and morale will suffer. The more we understand and can make our employees aware of the nature of emotional energy, the more congenial and productive our workplaces.

- **Mental Energy—**

This energy is generated when we use our minds to accomplish something. Our culture is dominated by mental energy.

We use mental energy when we play games that help educate us. We use it to design a beautiful building, a piece of art, or organize a great party. We can be very constructive with our mental energy. It's the energy that helped us develop all our technology and land men on the moon. We use this energy to do great things in the workplace. We use it to design software, create a hybrid car, or experiment to come up with new vaccines. Mental energy is also very helpful when dealing with very specific organizational processes, statistics, and financial situations in business.

Unfortunately, there are aspects of mental energy that make it susceptible to abuse. Because the mind uses the brain to run its functions, there is an electric energetic discharge that accompanies mental activity. This energy is measurable, and we are very attracted to it. It triggers our greed, and so we are more likely to want to create and hoard mental energy than we are any of the other energies. We can take mental energy to extremes. Many people are power hungry, and they use their mental energy to dominate situations from a place of thinking versus feeling. (They shut down feeling.) An extreme negative use of this energy shows up as mental bullying, degrading someone based on their assumed lack of intelligence, or withholding information in order to trip others up so that we can feel more powerful.

Mental energy is little understood, and so it's often misused. We have a tendency to use this energy more negatively than positively. Therefore, be on the lookout for the negative use of mental energy in the workplace. You know you are in the presence of very strong mental energy when the following criteria are all met simultaneously:

- The energy feels overtly aggressive; it feels harsh and

focused on a single goal or agenda.
- The energy feels very analytical, and has an unyielding force.
- The energy feels slippery, and moderately difficult to pin down.
- The levels of intensity are inconsistent.

To a great extent, Western culture runs on mental energy. When we over-rely on this energy we actually become more susceptible to illusion and delusion. This is because we tend to discount (or disparage) *feeling*. It's our ability to feel that actually helps us evaluate things, and thus avoid the trap of illusion.

Mental energy can also be blocked or depressed, for a variety of reasons. Mentally depressed people are listless and bored or have difficulty staying focused. We have a growing mental illness problem in the U.S. A significant percentage may actually be a depression of mental energy, rather than emotional energy. As with all our personal energies, mental energy is finite, and can be over-used.

If we are gifted with mental energy, we can use it in a positive way to help us understand and treat the mental problems that occur in business due to too much stress. Because mental energy is so dominant in our culture, being able to identify and channel it in a positive direction is advantageous to any business.

• The Energy of Human Dynamics—

Whenever humans interact we generate energy. That energy accumulates in a freestanding pool that we can tap into when we need to do something that has a high profile and involves other people. A political rally is a good example. We tap into that pool of human dynamic energy by thinking about the things that we share in common with others. This amplifies our individual energy, and creates a bridge to the other person. If you slow down and develop your sensitivity, you can feel this energy. It has a heavy, pushy, non-descript, and mysterious quality. Its specific origin is not evident.

Human dynamic energy comes into play in all business activities that involve working with people. It's especially important when we are conducting business transactions. Some individuals are gifted at being able to use this energy. They can read the energy of a group, organize it, and use it to accomplish something. Politicians use this energy to help them campaign, or enlist support for their ideas. Like all energies, it can be used constructively or destructively. The destructive use of this energy shows up as manipulation. Applying this energy to the business world in a constructive way can help us develop better teamwork in a project situation, conduct successful brainstorming sessions, and upgrade business products, for example.

- **Conflict Energy--**

Conflict energy is created whenever there is disagreement or fighting. This energy is around us all the time, because *there is not a time that humans are not in conflict with something*. We are always adding to, and taking away from this pool of conflict energy.

Conflict energy attracts us, because it's easy for us to access. We are easily enthralled by aggressive energetics. When we're in the flow of conflict energy there seem to be no boundaries, no set rules. We almost seem shielded from consequences. It's important to note that we can get addicted to conflict energy, because of the adrenal rush. People who instigate a lot of conflict do so because they want to be on a constant high. We often engage with—and feed—this pool of conflict energy. Here are some of the signs that indicate we're engaging with conflict energy:

- Our mood changes unexpectedly or abruptly.
- We find ourselves feeling suddenly defensive.
- We find ourselves either wanting to, or actually becoming

involved in situations of a combative nature, even when the issue isn't ours; we find ourselves jumping in when we were not invited.
- We feel like we need to be very critical about things that we don't have the ability to do anything about.
- We find ourselves wanting to control a situation, when it isn't our place to do so.
- We're participating in creating havoc.

We tend to use conflict energy to attain dominance over others. It's often used to gain political power, or to achieve a strategic edge in sports or advertising, for example. But conflict energy is not all bad; we can use this energy in a constructive way. In the business world, management can leverage conflict energy to work toward clarity about the causes of problems. It can be used to help diagnose production difficulties, for instance. Conflict is often symptomatic of a change that is trying to occur. By paying attention to the source of the tension, you can determine what new need or desire wants to emerge. This is important because the management of personnel often involves the resolution of conflict.

• Creative Energy/Creative Flow—

This is the energy involved in creative effort. Human beings are naturally creative, and we are always generating this energy, so it's always around us. Creative energy is a lot like conflict energy in that there is a constant standing pool of creative energy available to us. You can recognize creative energy by the following characteristics. Creative energy:

- Feels very motivational
- Feels very distracting and un-grounding
- Heightens your senses to dizzying levels
- Influences your sense of priorities
- Enthralls you, and keeps you unaware of anything other

than what you are focusing on
- Makes you susceptible to other creative processes

There are many constructive ways to draw upon and use this energy, and great things can happen in the workplace when this energy is used correctly. You can create award-winning advertising, a successful new product line, new software to solve a computer problem, or a new way to manage personnel problems. You can create a great exchange program with the surrounding community, or natural environment. You can use it to create solutions to social problems, such as developing a program to teach youth how to support their peers not to use drugs.

Unfortunately, the easy availability of creative energy means it can be misused or abused easily. For example, you can use this energy to con someone, or to convince someone to create a crime. People can also use their creative energy to tyrannize others, or to support their greed instead of using it to for more generative ends, such as environmental conservation or developing sustainable alternatives. The most important guideline to keep in mind is this: Creative energy should *not be used solely for self-serving purposes*.

Why do businesspeople need to understand creative energy? So much of what we do in business is creative, but we engage with this energy very unconsciously. Because there's so much creative energy being used in business, it's important to understand how to work with it. Say you're running an ad agency. Perhaps there's a tremendous creative flow going, but maybe the environment has become extreme; clients are starting to feel intimidated or coerced into campaigns that don't serve them. This can lead to loss of clients or a bad reputation. Perhaps the creative flow is blocked, and nothing's getting done. People can get very emotionally invested in their creative work, so emotional energy may be running high. Some people may even be exceptionally creative in support of their laziness. As a manager, you'll need to effectively manage the situation, and help these apparently "temperamental" people get back on track. Obviously, the use of this energy in the workplace needs to be monitored carefully. An understanding of the nature of creative energy can help you navigate these waters.

• The Energy of Personal and Group Imagery—

This energy is complex, so we will just be able to introduce it here. By "imagery" we mean the residue of our life experiences. When we engage in an activity, the memory of that activity is released to the open airwaves and accumulates around us as an energetic field. This imagery surrounds each of us individually. It also surrounds groups who have had shared experiences.

We are constantly perceiving and reacting to the imagery that people carry around with them in their electro-magnetic field or their emotional body, albeit unconsciously for the most part. For example, people may perceive your imagery as calming or chaotic. Depending upon our particular sensitivities, we will pick up on this residue visually (as images), physically (as a feeling, smell or taste), or even aurally (as sound). Each of us is attracted to certain kinds of imagery. It pulls us toward particular people or groups. We get involved with them so that we can bring some of their energy into our lives.

Our imagery is extremely important, because other people can sense it. Every business has its own imagery, and this affects how people perceive it. Therefore, it is advisable to consciously develop your business's imagery. You need to work not only on the public image you want to put forward, but on the energetics that surround that image as well You want to make sure you are not giving mixed signals. In addition, as the leader of the business, your personal imagery affects how people respond to both you and your business. You want to ensure that your personal imagery and that of your business complement (and not contradict) each other. We will discuss how to consciously create the image of your business in Volume 2.

Imagery energy also affects how the people in your business interact with each other. Groups within a business often generate imagery about themselves and others. This imagery can involve biases or prejudices about other groups or departments. This leads to negative dynamics that impede the business. The energy of group imagery can also be used constructively in business. When we want to inspire a group of people to accomplish a certain goal, we can use this energy to create a positive vision/image of what we want to accomplish. We can use imagery to help us energize and organize all kinds of groups: boards of directors, committees, advisory boards, governmental agencies, management teams, and work teams. A good understanding of the energetics of imagery can help us lead, train, and counsel people and resolve conflicts.

- **Spiritual Energy**—

This is the energy that comes forward when we are engaging with the sacred and/or the Divine. We use this energy to help us develop our personal philosophy about what is ethical and moral and to guide our everyday behaviors. It affects how we get along with others and shapes some of our personal routines.

There are some very good examples of the constructive use of spiritual energy. The Dalai Lama, Golda Meir, Mahatma Gandhi, and Jimmy Carter are all examples of individuals who have worked effectively with spiritual energy. Organizations that have a strong base in spiritual energy include the Salvation Army organization, the Sisters of Mercy, and the Cousteau Society.

As with any energy, it is subject to our extremist tendencies. We have to be very conscious about how we engage with this energy because it's often mis-used and abused. The Spanish Inquisition and religious persecutions of any kind are the most obvious examples of abuse. We also abuse spiritual energy when we exploit people's spiritual needs for personal gain. Many self-proclaimed "gurus" have done this.

The more we understand this energy, the better we can manage our employees and the human dynamics in the workplace. Whether we want it to or not, this energy comes into the workplace through our personnel. We practice good spiritual energy management by being sensitive to people's spiritual practices throughout the day, and by understanding how the lack of participating in these practices can adversely affect their work efficiency and personal behavior patterns. In addition, the more we understand this energy, the more we can be on the lookout for the abuse of this energy in the workplace. An example would be using our preference for certain kinds of spiritual energy to profile people for a job. This blocks our access to potentially eligible and highly qualified people, disrupting the flow of energy. This kind of behavior on the part of management can engender resentment and fear in employees; it leads to distrust and adversely affects loyalty. The importance of spiritual energy to business is greater than one may realize.

Working with Human Energies

We each have a unique energetic make-up. We are each endowed with all of these energies, but at different levels. Some people are particularly strong in certain energies, whereas others are weak in those energies. In addition, we all have a tendency to amplify our own energy by engaging with that of other people. We have a tendency to take them to extremes.

If you have a good understanding of these energies, you'll have an appreciation for people's energetic make-up, which is key to helping you manage them effectively. Below are some guidelines to help you recognize these different types of human energy.

- A person strong in **Personal (E-M) Energy** will tend to have a very strong presence, though they may be quiet. They will be very physically healthy, with a lot of stamina. People will be very energized by being around them. They are likely to be extraordinary healers, and may also be great manifestors. Examples include Theodore Roosevelt, Michael Jordan, and Clara Barton.

If someone pushes their personal E-M energy to the extreme, they will tend to be very self-centered, and self-involved. The signs would be that someone is concerned only about what works for them. Another sign is that they are very ambitious, but want success just for themselves. If someone is very low in personal energy, they may tend toward the extreme of martyrism.

• A person strong in **Human Dynamic Energy** will have an ability to tap into the human dynamic energy surrounding a situation. They're always asking themselves (not necessarily consciously), How does what I'm doing/saying work with this person or group? They will tend to be gifted politicians and/or mediators. Examples include Bill Clinton, Nelson Mandela, New Mexico Governor Bill Richardson, and Nancy Pelosi.

As with any energy, it can be used both positively and negatively. When someone who is strong in this energy uses it in a destructive manner, you'll see him or her trying to maneuver and manipulate situational dynamics to get more power. A person who is very low in this energy may tend to abdicate their power by surrendering to the will of others.

• A person strong in **Conflict Energy** tends to become involved in a lot of conflicts. In extreme cases, they may even seem to thrive on trauma or drama. It's not unusual to see such people provoking conflicts. In contrast, someone very low in conflict energy will tend to avoid conflicts. This, too, can be taken to an extreme.

It's very possible for someone with a strong, innate knowledge of conflict energy to channel it positively. They may become a counselor, negotiator, or mediator who helps others to work through conflicts. Reformed convicts who work with troubled kids are examples. Another example is Jimmy Santiago Baca, a former prisoner who is now a poet. Santiago Baca's poetry expresses pain and suffering, but also celebrates the human spirit.

• A person strong in **Creative Energy** is always looking for new ways to do things. They are inventive, and can become easily bored. They can be temperamental. Examples include Benjamin Franklin, Frida Kahlo, Leonard Bernstein, Ando Hiroshige, and Gloria Steinem.

People who take their creative energy to an extreme might be easily distracted. They may have a lot of ideas, but lack the discipline to follow through on their ideas. At the other extreme are people who display no creative fire, and seem lackluster.

• A person strong in **Kinetic Energy** will be active, physically robust, and "on the go." Oftentimes, these people are athletes. They prefer physically active work, and enjoy breaking a sweat. They do poorly at sit-down jobs. Examples include Rudolph Nureyev and Mohammad Ali.

In the extreme, there are people who just can't sit still. At the other extreme are people who seem listless.

• A person strong in **Emotional Energy** will be very aware of emotions, both their own and others'. They own their emotions and show them. This does not mean, however, that such people are what we call "emotional." Their comfort with emotions means that they can work effectively with their emotions, without drama. Jay Leno is probably a good example.

It is when emotional energy is taken to an extreme that you find people who are emoting all the time and who are prone to dramatic displays. At the other extreme, there are people who repress their emotional energy. They may appear extremely stoical; they may refuse to acknowledge any emotions, either their own or those of others.

• A person strong in **Mental Energy** will tend to be curious, alert, and focused. They are "always thinking." They are innovative, when creative energy is also present. They are often determined, and can be stubborn. Examples include Alan Greenspan, Hillary Clinton, and Charlie Rose. An example of a person with both strong mental and creative energy is Marie Curie.

When taken to an extreme, people high in mental energy are constantly at the edge of every mental process, every new idea. They are probably very competitive. They are always testing: How smart am I? They may be "power hungry," and use their mental prowess negatively, to dominate others. At the other extreme, you find people who are mentally lazy and/or intellectually incurious or shut down.

• A person strong in **Spiritual Energy** is comfortable with spiritual topics and spirituality in general. They tend to practice their spirituality outwardly, and let people know about its importance to them. Ministers in general exemplify this energy.

A luminous exemplar is Agnes Baker Pilgrim, a Takelma Tribal Elder. Baker Pilgrim is one of the 13 Indigenous Grandmothers, and is the oldest living female left of the Rogue River Indians, who lived in Southern Oregon for over 20,000 years. At age 45, she was called to the spiritual path. "Handed down from my people was a story that the only duty left to us from the ancient ones was the duty of prayer. So I became a prayer person," she says. Baker Pilgrim prays for "the voiceless," for endangered species and polluted rivers. She encourages us to raise our voices to save Mother Earth (and ourselves). [13]

People who don't follow a moderate path with their spiritual energy are often evangelistic. They try to convert others. At the other extreme are people who treat the spiritual path with derision.

• A person strong in **Personal/Group Imagery Energy** will easily tune into the imagery of a person or situation. They sense a situation on all levels, with depth. These people are intuitive and are natural organizers of groups. Examples include Carl Sagan, Stephen Spielberg, the psychic Allison Dubois, and Madeleine Albright.

At the extreme, there are people who can only focus on their own personal imagery. They are very involved with their personal experiences, and talk a lot about them. They may have the capacity to pull you into their world such that you lose yourself. At the other extreme are people who just cannot relate to imagery at all.

As we've said, humans have a natural tendency toward extremism. This is true with respect to our use of energy. Unfortunately, many people who are gifted with a particular energy will use that particular energy excessively. At the other end of the spectrum, people who are weak in a particular energy will demonstrate little of that energy, and are reticent to work with it. If pushed too far, however, these people can have an extreme reaction. Imagine, if you will, a person low in conflict energy who is goaded into conflict by others who are strong in this energy. The results can be devastating for all.

Unless we are taught how to work with our own energetic make-up, our natural tendency toward extremism tends to take over. Moderation is the key. We need to learn how to moderate our energies. We best learn this skill by working with an elder or some other person who models moderation, and thus can serve as an exemplar to us. Through workshops or counseling we can learn to be more conscious of our personal energetic make-up. This will help us to recognize when we are going to extremes so we can get the help we need to transition out of that extremism.

Implications for Business

Why is an understanding of these energies important to business?

Workplaces are energy fields that need conscious management. The climate of the workplace is a product of all the different energetics within it. For example, people can bring a great deal of emotional energy into the workplace; a workplace can be charged with the energy of conflict. If we understand these energies and can recognize them, we'll be in a better position to help people manage their energy. A working knowledge of energy can help us:

- Pay attention to individual and organizational energetics when hiring, building teams, making decisions, etc., to ensure we have the most suitable energetic structure. We all have preferences for certain energies and people tend to hire to their preferences because that increases comfort. But a more important question to ask is, what energy is best for the business? Here's an obvious example. If we have a bias toward people who have a lot of creative energy, and we're not aware of that, we could end up with a group that can generate great ideas. But without people who can actually produce the product, which requires a different kind of energy, our business will flounder.

- Support and foster the constructive use of these different energies. We'll be able to direct certain powerful energies (like emotional or conflict energy) so that they are used most constructively and productively. This might mean giving people with a lot of creative energy the opportunity to come up with new ways of doing business. Then, we can give the people with a lot of mental energy the challenge of working out the logistics. Those people who are gifted with physical energy, such as mechanics, line managers, and delivery people, put the logistics into action.

- Create or open new channels for energy to flow. When we discover a business issue or problem, we can use our knowledge of these different kinds of energies to parse/analyze what kinds of energies are being blocked. Then, we can create solutions that free up that blocked energy, and set it flowing again. This might mean creating new policies, a new team, or a new project, product, or service.

- Read the energetics of people or groups, and respond accordingly. For example, if you are sensitive to the E-M fields of your employees, you can recognize when your people are approaching "burn out." You'll avoid over-using our own personal energy, and that of others, as this can lead to health complications and even death. You'll also be able to assess whether your personal energy, or that of others, is being abused in some way.

- Moderate and balance the deployment of these different energies so that they are not taken to extremes. In general, the culture of modern business tends toward extremism, so we need to work consciously at tending the energetic profile of our workplaces so they do not become extreme environments.

The Circle and Energy

The linear pattern has little to offer with respect to helping us work effectively with energy. As we've discussed, its nature is inherently consuming of energy. Of all the blueprints, the Circle is the most versatile with respect to energy. The Circle is, itself, an energy pattern—the primary energy pattern in the cosmos. It is boundless enough to hold, contain, and sustain many other types of energy. And, because it is a part of everything, it can relate to all different kinds of energy. When we use it as the underlying blueprint for a business, the Circle can help us organize, manage, and develop our energetic resources. The Circle can do this because of its innate gifts: relationship, movement, focus, balance, and moderation, in particular.

The Circle can help us orchestrate the various energies in our organizations so they flow in a constructive and balanced way, creating a harmonious flow and vibrant culture. Creative energy, for example, can spin off in multiple directions; human dynamic energy can easily devolve into chaos. When you introduce Circle energy into a group dynamic, however, it promotes moderation. A leader who understands how to work with Circle energy can use it to restore order and refocus the group. We will discuss how in more detail in Volume 2.

All of the energies we have just discussed do not tell the whole story. They are only individualized expressions of something much more profound, awesome, and boundless: Universal Energy. We turn to this topic next.

Chapter Four
The Circle and Universal Energy

If everything in the universe happens in cycles, what does that mean for our human existence?

Although early indigenous people did not have the conceptual language to express intellectual understandings as we do now, they knew that the Circle was part of nature, and that we are also part of nature. Without modern science and without philosophical debate, they came to understand that human beings need to work with, and be a part of, the larger Circle. All wisdom traditions point toward this fundamental truth. There is a pattern to the flow of the universe: it flows in a circle. It follows that when human activities flow in a circular manner, they receive tremendous support from the universe. Aligning with this Universal Energy flow is key to lasting happiness, success, and peace. This wisdom is applicable to business.

Universal Energy is the source of all other energies and everything that exists. Without it, there would be no sun, no Earth, no life, no universe. It's the background energy upon which everything plays. It's the "juice" that animates everything that is. It's transcendent and infinitely creative. It is always moving, always flowing.

This Universal Energy is around all of us. It may be in active, physical form, such as fire, wind, or jet propulsion. It may be in the form of latent, dormant, potential energy, such as an unlit candle, a turbine engine at rest, or even a table or a rock.

The concept of Universal Energy can be quite difficult to grasp, because it's so nebulous. We can't see it, but we can feel it. It is hard to describe. It is hard to rationalize. It's so vast and infinite that we have a hard time grasping the entirety of it. What are signs that we're in touch with Universal Energy? We feel something much larger than us, something that connects us to everything else that exists. You may also experience:

- A series of light fragrances that seem to periodically float by you (a mixture of fruity, rose/cinnamon, fresh evergreen, and damp earthy/woody and moist)

- A slight sweet and sour taste (*i.e.,* the "nectar of the throat," felt in a deep experience of yoga)

- A quick movement; the faint sound of a light wind or something going by very fast and brushing you

- Feelings of being firmly but gently pushed or falling through space with no end in sight

- A sense of mystery and enchantment, simultaneously

Practices like meditation, prayer, and yoga can put us in touch with this energy, but when we experience these things, we usually tell ourselves it's our imagination and tend to ignore it. It may not be wise to do so.

Universal Energy is the most powerful and creative force in the universe. This energy is *always available to us*. We can call upon it to support us in our creative endeavors. All that is required is that we align with it, meaning we enter into its flow, without resistance or trying to control it.

When we are able to align with Universal Flow we experience

an unprecedented degree of support. In aligning with this greater flow, we are able to *transcend our human limitations*. This is what we mean when we say we are "in the zone," or "in the flow." Research in the field of psychology has validated this phenomenon. We enter into this state when we become a clear channel. Then, Universal Energy flows through us, and lifts us at the same time. In a sense, the universe is working through us. We often experience fulfillment and sublime joy in this state. Universal Energy is so helpful and supportive, that reliance on force becomes unnecessary.

Since Universal Energy is available to support any and all human creative endeavors, we can enlist it to help us build and run a business. If we want to have a sustainable energy source for our endeavors—one that is powerful and virtually unlimited—we can choose to base our efforts in Universal Energy. In short, Universal Energy can be our most important business partner and resource.

When we set about to build or manage a business, then, we have an important choice to make. We can choose to operate on the basis of Universal Flow, or we can choose to operate solely on the basis of personal energy. It's a very important choice. It is one that we make all the time, generally without our full awareness.

The Lure of Personal Energy

Our current Western, linear approach tends to favor our conducting business on the basis of personal energy. It's entirely possible to do this. All human beings are innately creative; this is part of our personal energetic toolkit. Proceeding this way, however, has some important drawbacks that we should understand in order to make an informed choice. For one, it can be thrilling in short spurts, but it can also be exhausting. Relying solely upon our personal energy can leave us physically and mentally depleted. We can "burn out." Many entrepreneurs find themselves in this situation. Our personal energy is human-based, and therefore it's limited and finite. When our personal energy wanes, we can shore it up by commandeering the energy of others.

This puts us on a constant search for new sources of energy. This pursuit requires our constant attention, and so it actually drains us of energy as well. Sometimes, other people give us their energy willingly, but many times we try to coerce it from them by seducing or dominating them.

The more we rely on personal energy to fuel our endeavors, the more our approach becomes consumptive of others and ourselves. We start behaving in ways that actually contradict Universal Flow, which produces harmful effects on others, the earth and future generations, and even ourselves. Ultimately, this is not sustainable, but it's part-and-parcel of the linear way.

Leadership and Energy

Before we leave the topic of personal energy, we need to explain its relationship to leadership. We have a tendency to associate leadership with a quality known as *charisma*.

"Charisma" is the word we use to denote a particular type of personal electro-magnetic energy. Charisma is actually a combination of creative life force energy and sexual energy. All human beings possess creative life force energy as a necessary part of survival. This is the fire that enables us to create something, whether a piece of art, a marvelous dinner, or a beautiful building. The human vessel also comes with sexual energy, which fuels the procreative drive and the act of sex that goes with it. Sexual energy has a whole different flow and imagery than creative life force energy. It's the combination of the two that gives charisma its power.

The sexual energy that lies at the base of charismatic power makes it inherently seductive. This is why charismatic people are so attractive. The combination of these two energies can be volatile, chaotic, and potentially dangerous. It means that the true motivations of a charismatic leader are often muddy and difficult to discern (even by themselves). Internal clarity is generally an issue for these types of people. This internal chaos alarms them, but they lack the tools to distill the confusion. Often, they push ahead anyway, coming up with rationalizations as to why they're doing something. Partly, they do this to convince themselves that they're OK.

A charismatic person relies *only* on their personal, human, and physical energy. This is very tiring and draining, because human energy is finite; it needs to be continuously re-charged. This is why charismatic leaders have to feed off the energy of others. It is why followers find that charismatic leaders must be stroked continuously, which is draining to the followers.

The followers of charismatic leaders may feel like they're focused, when in reality they're in the throes of a chaotic and unpredictable energy. Sexual energy is aggressive, coercive, and unstable. As a consequence, a charismatic leader's followers will also tend to be volatile and aggressive. Making matters worse, charisma tends to exert its strongest effect on people who already have tendencies toward emotional instability.

Leaders are *most effective and truly powerful when their energy base transcends the personal, human, physical plane.* The alternative energetic format for leadership is called *magnetic energy*. Magnetic energy draws on both personal creative life force energy and the transcendent creative life force energy that comes from the Universe. There is no sexual energy component, so it's not as seductive or aggressive. But even more importantly, because it has a base in Universal Energy, magnetic energy is self-renewing. A magnetic leader can re-charge by simply reconnecting with Universal Flow. They do not need to feed off the adulation of followers. In addition, the actions of a magnetic leader will be commensurate with the flow of Universal Energy because they will use Universal Laws and Principles (which we will discuss in the next chapter) as their guidelines. In particular, the motivation of a magnetic leader will altruistic, meaning these leaders will want to discover and do that which is best for all concerned, including themselves. Their motivation will not seem confusing; it will be clean and clear.

You can use this knowledge of energetics to help you identify people who have leadership potential, *i.e.,* people who have magnetic energy in their personal make-up. It can also help you avoid putting charismatic leaders in power positions unless the need is only short-term, and understood as such.

Being in the Flow of Universal Energy

Like all energy, Universal Energy is always in movement. We have referred to this constant movement as Universal Flow. One of the fundamental premises of this book is that life will be most rewarding, successful, and sustainable when our actions align with this flow; this includes the way we conduct business. We always have the option of choosing to conduct business solely on the basis of personal energy so, as businesspeople, this presents us with perhaps the most important choice we can make. In order to make an informed choice, we need to understand the nature of Universal Flow, as it has some characteristics that make it quite challenging for humans.

Universal Energy is the source of everything, and everything is made up of Universal Energy. Universal Energy is the progenitor and the guardian of the Whole. Therefore, Universal Energy is supportive of all that exists. Consequently, it always flows in the direction of that which is *best for the whole*. It cannot do otherwise.

Universal Energy is supportive of all that exists, equally. The flow of Universal Energy is not biased toward any particular faction or species; this includes humans. Universal Flow is *not human-centric*. This is challenging to us. Out of our insecurity, we want to be at the center, on the top, and to be preferred. We find this idea threatening, so we'll protest and resist at the beginning. But, in time, this knowledge actually has an infinitely calming effect, for it restores us to our appropriate relationship with all that exists. Once we connect with the fundamental truth of that relationship the stress and strain that accompanies trying to be more than everything else falls away, and serenity begins to take its place.

We must also recognize that Universal Flow has both constructive and destructive aspects. These are both equally valuable and necessary. Sometimes, destruction is necessary for the overall health of the whole. An example of this is the way a tree grows and supports its surrounding environment. It provides food, homes, and temporary shelter for many species and keeps the soil intact. Eventually, the tree will die, and it will be deconstructed (destroyed) by nature. We may mourn the loss of a beloved tree, but in its disintegration, it becomes a protective nursery, providing nutrients for the next generation of trees, shrubs, and grasses. Because we humans have a limited view, it is difficult for us to judge whether an event is "good" or "bad" in this larger, universal sense. We just don't always see the whole picture.

Another aspect of Universal Flow is that it is continuously shifting and changing in order to support everything equally. This can seem very chaotic to us humans, so it can trigger our fears. When we're afraid, we tend to fight with Universal Flow and/or try to control it. That takes us out of the Flow. It is key to understand that Universal Energy favors moderation and balance. It flows into things, people, and situations that are in a state of moderation and balance. When we practice moderation and balance we become a clear, static-free conduit into which Universal Energy easily flows.

The process of continuously moving into moderation and balance is especially challenging for us humans. For one, the universe is always changing, so the process of finding moderation and balance is continuous and dynamic. Most of us have probably experienced the sheer joy and sense of efficacy that comes from feeling in tune with and supported by the Universe. It is so wonderful that we try to hold onto it, and we're upset when it seems to disappear. We wonder what's wrong with us. The answer is: Nothing. We are merely succumbing to the illusion of attainable perfection. We will fall out of the Flow at times; when we do, it is an opportunity for learning.

Another challenge comes from the fact that we tend to get emotionally invested in how things are supposed to be (from our human perspective). Because we have been so influenced by the linear pattern, we are used to taking control and forcing things to happen. We tend to have expectations of immediate gain on any energy we expend. We are often disappointed. When things aren't going as planned, we get frustrated. When we're frustrated, we tighten up and constrict, unconsciously shutting down our access to Universal Energy. Before we know it, we're in a downward spiral. We become even more stuck and frustrated. As our insecurity kicks into high gear, we grasp at quick, destructive processes rather than slower, more constructive ones. We get involved with our human factors: laziness, extremism, emotionality, etc. We may start blaming and projecting our problems onto others. The more we do this, the more we choke off our access to Universal Flow. Pretty soon, we're completely on our own, working solely from our human, personal and/or group energy. Our energy source is now finite and limited—not universal. If things continue not to flow the way we want, we can become resigned or apathetic. We lose our motivation and our manifestation abilities come to a dead stop. Sound familiar?

We can't control Universal Flow, but we can learn to work with it. This is key to human happiness—and business success. Learning to work with Universal Energy requires us to be patient with ourselves—and with the way that the Universal works. We must have the patience to allow things to come together of their own accord. This may not always happen the way we want it to, or on the schedule we want. Our newfound patience will be amply rewarded, however. Generally the Universe comes up with far better options and solutions than we could have ever imagined. The outcomes will take a little longer, but they will be much longer-lasting. The energy we put into our efforts will never be lost; it will come back to us in full measure, in due time. This is a more indirect, but much more rewarding way to conduct our businesses and our lives.

The Circle as Our Primary Energy Tool

The Circle is the most powerful tool we have to help us stay in Universal Flow. The Circle is infinite, and so the energy that flows within it is also infinite. This connects the Circle to Universal Flow at its root and foundation. In turn, we humans are connected to

Universal Flow through the Circle, which is within us, at *our* root and foundation.

The Circle can act as a kind of "ambassador" or "go between" for us. Because of its very nature, it is in touch with Universal Flow and its natural cycles. The Circle also has its own energy. Circle Energy is more human-friendly than Universal Flow, so it is easier for us humans to relate to. Because the Circle is a non-human form of energy, it can help ameliorate our human-ness. This also helps put us in the flow of Universal Energy.

The Circle, being a part of everything, can act as a bridge between everything in the Universe and its Flow. Because it can relate to and contain so many different energies, the Circle has a tremendous wealth of knowledge about all of the energy dynamics we have discussed in this and the previous chapters. All of these qualities contribute to making it our primary tool for working effectively with energy. And still, there is more.

The Circle as a Universal Blueprint

As early humans pondered and observed the world around them, they came to some very important understandings. They saw that the constantly repeating Circle of nature contained a pattern. They saw this pattern in the rising and setting of the sun each day. They saw the same pattern repeated in the cycle of the seasons. They saw that human life paralleled this same pattern: from nothingness to conception, to birth and vibrant life, to maturity, to death and then rebirth in a different form. This repeating pattern moved from the dark to the light and back again. From the un-manifest and formless, it surged into form: manifestation. It sprouted, blossomed, swelled, and roared; it faded and relinquished itself again into the formless. This pattern recurred, repeated, and persisted. Sometimes the pattern could be easily seen in a day, a year, or a single lifetime; sometimes it took generations to comprehend its span. The completion of some cycles, they realized, might be beyond human comprehension: too vast, remote and exalted. But the pattern was always there, just beyond the human eye, shimmering with mystery.

As ancient humans studied the circular process of energy flow, their understanding grew. They saw that this pattern was made up of different and unique energies that came into play at different stages as the process unfolded. Over time, each of these energies came to be associated with a compass direction. They used the Circle to hold and express this understanding.

There are four primary energies, just as there are the four aspects of a day, four seasons, and four major stages of life. These are represented by the Cardinal Directions:

- The **East** direction is where the sun rises. This direction represents the energy associated with the start of the day, spring, conception, birth, and the seed. It's the place of new beginnings, where we are called to commence a new journey.

- The **South** represents the energy associated with noon (mid-day), summer, and young adulthood. It's about growth, work, apprenticing to our chosen venture, and producing the fruits of our labor.

- The **West** is where the sun sets. Its energy is that of late-afternoon/early evening, fall, maturity, sunset, and harvest. It's a time for reflection and evaluation, a place of assessing our progress and for refinement. It is where living creatures teach what we have learned. It is about giving thanks and gratitude.

- The **North** direction represents midnight, winter, and elderhood. In winter, fields go fallow, and activity occurs underground, away from the curious eye. In the North, we prepare to complete our present individual life—with an accompanying sense of accumulated experience and wisdom. We surrender to the cyclical nature of all of life. It's a place of stillness. Here, all sentient beings develop the courage to undertake the passage to death: the return to the formless. Its energy is about transition/transformation, resting, spiritual connection and evolution. Here we resolve things through making decisions, re-committing, or releasing/letting go of that which no longer works. These actions restore equilibrium. Those with knowledge of the North direction have the ability to mentor others.

- The **Center** of the Circle is the most powerful energy of all. It holds the larger perspective, the knowledge of the whole. Its energy is visionary, and its breadth infinite. It represents connection with Universal Flow, continuous movement, and ongoing transition. The Center reminds us to step back and look at the larger perspective: to look at how our intended actions will affect all concerned today, and in future generations.

Arranged around a circle, these understandings create a profound—yet extremely accessible—system of meaning and value.

The Complementary Aspects of the Circle:
Cycle of the day
Seasons
Lifecycle
Survival
Spiritual Path

North:
Midnight
Winter
Elderhood
Resting & Recharge
Mentor

West:
Sunset
Autumn
Middle Age
Assessment
Teacher

Center:
Visionary
Infinite
Universal Flow
Transition

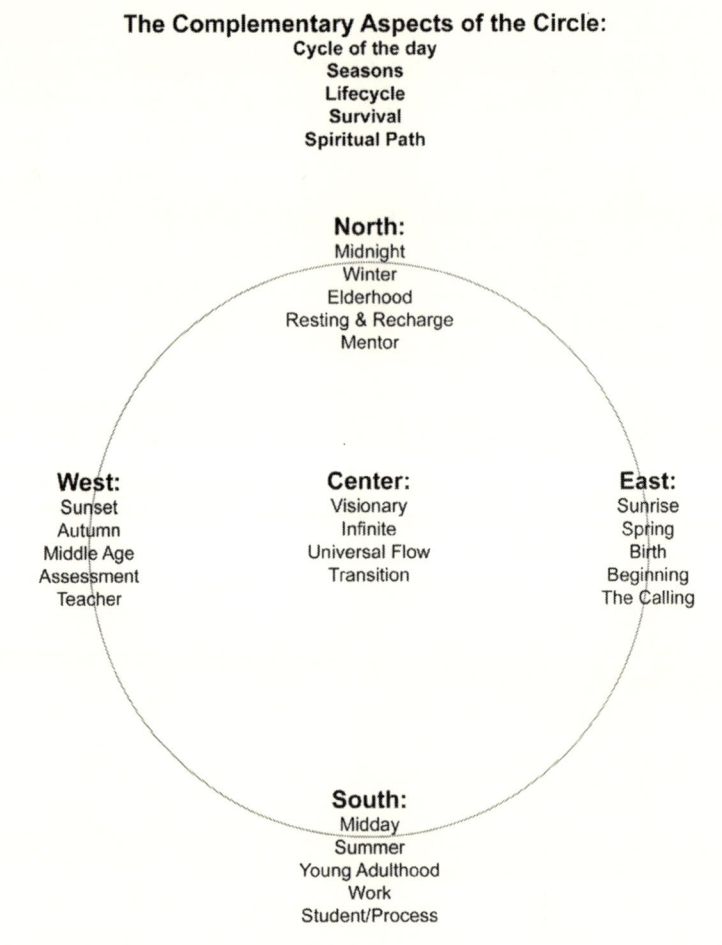

East:
Sunrise
Spring
Birth
Beginning
The Calling

South:
Midday
Summer
Young Adulthood
Work
Student/Process

Figure 1

In addition to the energies represented by the Cardinal directions there are also energies represented by the four Quadrant Directions: Southeast, Southwest, Northwest, and Northeast. The four quadrant directions represent *transitional* energies. They support the work of the cardinal energies. These energies are subtler, yet they are equally important. These quadrant direction energies are as follows:

- The **Southeast**, which is the energy mid-morning and late spring. It's the energy of childhood, a time when crucial first, solid, and loyal alliances are formed. It represents the energy involved in accumulating resources, and knowledge in preparation for a productive adulthood.

- The **Southwest,** which is the energy of mid-afternoon and late summer. It represents the energy of maturing, and taking time to start evaluating the output of the preceding interval. It's the place where we put things to the test, and begin to learn what works and what doesn't.

- The **Northwest,** which is the energy of mid-evening and late fall. In human terms, the Northwest represents the beginning of the senior years process. It's about reassessment, and dealing with the reality of change. In this place, we seek to create greater balance. We do so by taking stock and preparing for resolution.

- The **Northeast,** which is the energy of late night, just preceding dawn, and late winter. It represents the period after retirement. It's a time for sharing and evolving on an even deeper level. It's the energy of completion, in preparation for ending an old cycle and beginning anew.

As humankind's understanding of the Circle evolved it became a universal blueprint, a kind of "universal compass" that we used to provide structure, meaning, and direction for our lives.

The Universal Circle Blueprint and Universal Flow

This Universal Blueprint describes an energy pattern that permeates All, in terms that humans can understand. The Circle is a map of a process that is repeated over and over again in the cycles of nature.

~ Business Revolution through Ancestral Wisdom ~

**The Circle:
A Universal Blueprint**

North:
Creating equilibrium through decision-making & releasing

Northwest:
Creating balance

Northeast:
Completing & preparing for a new beginning

West:
Assessing & evaluating

Center:
Gaining the larger perspective

East:
Inspiration, ideas, visions, new beginnings

Southwest:
Testing & filtering

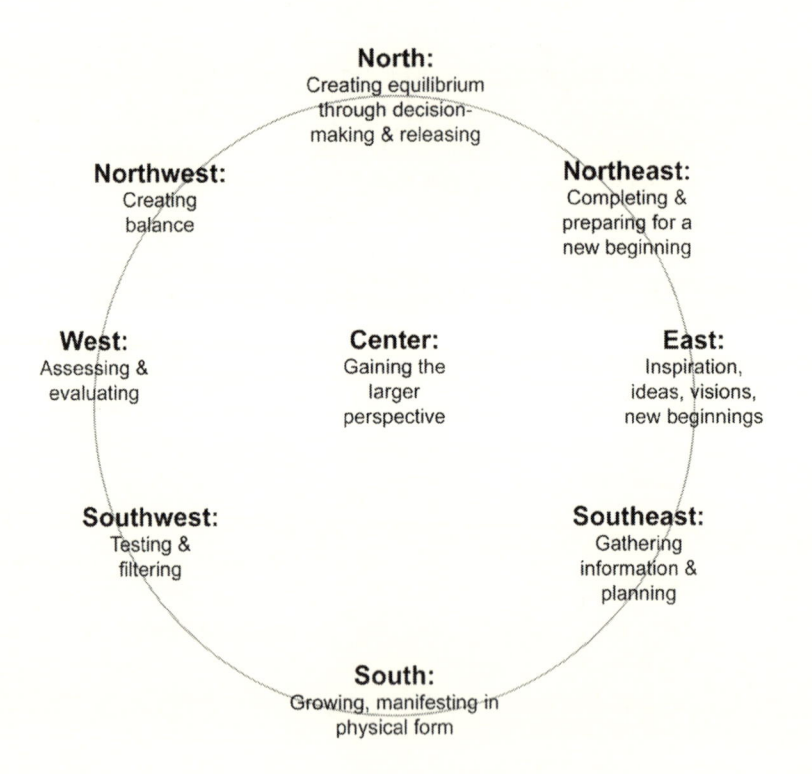

Southeast:
Gathering information & planning

South:
Growing, manifesting in physical form

Figure 2

    The Circle and the nine Directions represent nine different types of energy. These constitute a holistic process. This process replicates the processes of nature and is applicable to all human endeavors. When we engage with this process we put ourselves in the flow of the Universe.

    The Circle process begins with an idea, vision, or inspiration (East). It guides us to gather the necessary resources (Southeast), and bring our idea into physical manifestation (South). Then, we listen to immediate feedback (Southwest), and adjust accordingly.

~ 86 ~

~ Business Revolution through Ancestral Wisdom~

Moving on, we enter a period of reflection and assessment (West), and seek to make changes in order to achieve greater balance (Northwest). We make decisions, and release what doesn't work in order to achieve equilibrium (North). Then we complete; we create closure on the old cycle by sharing abundance received with those who collaborated in our success (Northeast). Before starting anew we go to the Center, which connects us to the larger perspective. There we take full measure of our course, and re-commit to the future. A new cycle then begins, building upon the knowledge obtained in the previous cycle.

As both blueprint and compass, the Circle can help us find our direction and guide our lives, as well as our work. As a process, it is complete and comprehensive in a way that linear processes are not, because it helps us deal with the wholeness of things. It enables us to work with multiple dimensions of wholeness. The Circle acknowledges that all of these functions are important to the whole. The Center helps us to integrate all the functions by asking us to take on the role of witness, leader, and questioner.

The Circle is a structure for a process that is powerful, natural, universal, and innately holistic. It shows us how the "Power of the World" moves. It shows us that it consists of rising and falling, taking and giving back. It's yang transmuting into yin and back again. It is the waxing and waning phases of the moon, and all of life. All of these different energies are necessary to the Circle process. And of these different energies are hosted by the Circle; they compliment and fill out its innate abilities. In this way, this Universal Blueprint exemplifies the acceptance of diversity, the valuing different strengths and talents for the betterment of all. It's the profound integration of all of these energies that gives the Circle its resonant power, whose wisdom is infinite.

Chapter Five
The Guidelines:
Universal Laws & Principles

Ah, not to be cut off,
Not through the slightest partition
Shut out from the law of the stars.
The inner—what is it?
If not intensified sky,
Hurled through with birds and deep
With the winds of homecoming.
-Rainer Maria Rilke

How should we live? How should we humans live so that we are in harmony with the universe? How does the universe really work? What are the underlying laws and principles that govern it?

Modern science is pursuing the latter two questions, while religion attempts to answer the first. But the two fields seem worlds apart. It was not always so.

So-called "primitive" people also asked these questions. They knew these questions were important. They lived in close quarters with each other. They knew from experience that human beings have a tendency to fall out of harmony with themselves, their fellow creatures, and all the other beings of the Earth. They knew that humans had the capacity for violence, cruelty, and self-centeredness. They knew that this part of our humanness had taken them to the brink of extinction. They sensed that human beings are complex, and that complexity is both a gift and a curse. It takes us outside ourselves, and it challenges us to continuously repair ourselves, to restore ourselves to harmony. For humans, finding balance is an ongoing, perpetual process—and we need help.

Not everyone understood this, of course. As with every group and every generation, there were only a few who had the courage—or ability—to face the true nature of their humanness, and to seek wisdom about how to live. These were people who believed that the lands upon which they lived and the heavens above them were their teachers. As modern man has set about taming and consuming—even destroying—nature in order to feel safe and masterful, these ancestors set out to learn from her. They closely observed nature, sensing that the patient study of her ways would reveal the keys to the mystery, the "law of the stars." They accumulated knowledge about their experience. Over time, that knowledge seasoned into wisdom. These became the Elders, the Keepers of Wisdom, and the shamans. They were venerated, and people sought them out for counsel and wisdom. In turn, they took on the responsibility of becoming living exemplars.

Over time, each passing generation added to this foundational knowledge. As this wisdom accumulated, it evolved, as is the nature of wisdom. At certain moments in history, the knowledge coalesced. As it did, it gave rise to spiritual traditions, religions, and other belief systems. Many of these are on the earth today, competing for our allegiance. Sometimes along the way our human understanding faltered. Sometimes political maneuvering intervened. Sometimes the original ideas were lost, or changed, or re-shaped. Some things were emphasized more than others. That is why these belief systems differ. But the roots are the same.

In this chapter, we illuminate a set of universal truths. Together with the Rights of Beingness (delineated in the next chapter), these Universal Laws and Principles provide guidance for human beings about how to think and act in order to align with the flow of Universal Energy.[14] By aligning our human actions we improve, we are more successful, and we taste the joy of acting in harmony with the Universe (a most delicious byproduct!).

The Universal Laws and Principles can guide us in how to conduct business. Business is then *supported by Universal Flow, as well.* They are the collective description of our deepest and truest understandings of how the universe works, of how we are to interact with the greater whole. They are based on close observation of nature and experiential knowledge about what works and what doesn't work for ongoing sustainability. Our goal here is to revivify and reinstate this root wisdom, so that it can be used as a foundation for the conduct of business. Our intention is to articulate them in a way that is universal, that transcends any particular religion, philosophy, or ownership by any one group or person, and to make them accessible to all. This is not dogma, but a work-in-progress, and a gift from the heart.

Expressed with the help of the Circle, these are some of the Universal Laws and Principles that are most relevant to business:

~ Business Revolution through Ancestral Wisdom ~

The Beginning Circle of Universal Laws & Principles

North:
Laws of Transformation & Transmutation

Northwest:
Principle of Equitable Exchange

Northeast:
Law of Cooperation & Principle of Releasing

West:
Law of Transition

Center:
Law of Evolution

East:
Law of the Right To Be; Principles of Humility & Acceptance

Southwest:
Principle of Compassion

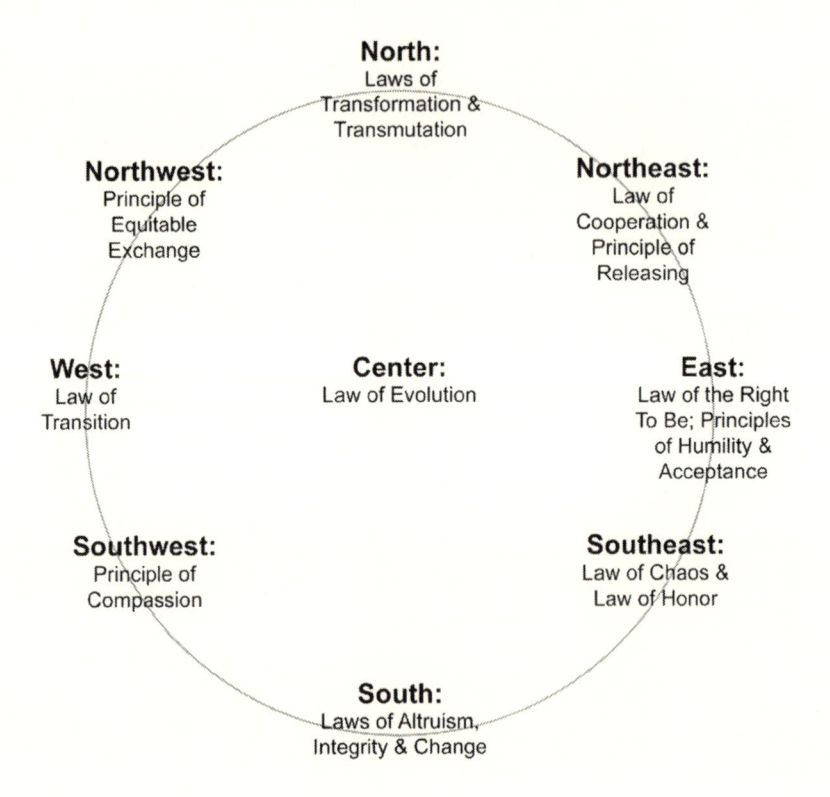

Southeast:
Law of Chaos & Law of Honor

South:
Laws of Altruism, Integrity & Change

Figure 3

The Circle, with its nine directions, acts as a bridge to help us with these laws and principles. The energy in each of the directions helps us humans relate to and understand the laws and principles associated with each particular direction. Sometimes we need the guidance of more than one universal law or principle to guide us in the proper enactment of these energies. Hence, some directions house multiple laws and/or principles. We'll now discuss each.

East: The Right to Be

As we humans understand it: *Everything that exists has the right to exist because it is a part of the whole.*

The Right to Be is the foundation. All the other laws and principles flow out of the Right to Be.

The Universal Law of the Right to Be says that everything in the universe—every being, every creature, every group, every species, every object, every action, every particle, every thought, concept, emotion, belief—has the right to exist. Put another way, there is nothing in the universe that does *not* have the right to exist. It's certainly not up to us humans to determine what has the right to exist, and what doesn't. Everything that exists is made up of Universal Energy; it's the source and origin of everything. Therefore, everything that exists is all part of the whole. Everything is one. The ancients understood this for millennia. Astrophysicists now have the physical proof: Everything that exists is made of stardust, literally.

In practice, the Right to Be means we must consciously give everything, human and non-human, the right to exist—including *ourselves* (and all the various parts of ourselves). The Right to Be is the basic starting place for all relationships. We must be open and receptive to others, and to their ideas, if we want our relationships to be successful.

Living in accordance with the Right to Be challenges humans. Historically, human beings have had a very difficult time giving this right to beings, ideas, or people we don't like or agree with. Many of our social and political struggles involve the question of whether we can give a group or an idea the right to exist amongst us. By looking at human history through this lens we see it as a series of struggles by individuals, groups, nations, and races for the Right to Be, and the right to be accorded equal treatment under the law. But legal treatment is only part of the picture. The Right to Be must be manifested in our daily interactions with all others things and beings, including those we fear, don't like, or don't understand.

Why is living in accordance with the Right to Be so difficult for us? It's difficult because, as a creature, we have a lot of insecurity regarding our place in creation. While we like to see ourselves as the pinnacle of creation, we have a buried awareness that we are not the strongest, fastest, or fiercest of creatures. We doubt our own worthiness even as we doubt the worthiness of others. Subconsciously, we question who and what we are, and what our place in the universe is. This is why the most difficult challenge many of us will face is *giving ourselves* the Right to Be.

This is part of the human dilemma. The cure is to choose not to drive our insecurity away, since it's built into us, but to accept it as a natural part of our human condition. By going *toward* our insecurity we can extend to everything in the universe the Right to Be.

The reward for living in accordance with the universal law of the Right to Be is that it opens us to the flow of Universal Energy. When you embrace the Right to Be, and give up any prejudice you may have toward some person, thing, situation, concept, or other, that act in and of itself dissipates blockages in the flow of energy. You can perceive things starting to run, work, or feel better. If we truly acknowledge that every being on the planet, including the Earth itself, has the Right to Be, we step into a different universe. It is one that is infused with a deep reverence for all beings, and a true humility in the presence of others. We would enter into a new relationship with the universe. We would have a sense of the proper order of things, and we would experience our own right to be honored and accepted by others merely because we exist.

East: The Principle of Humility

As we humans understand it: *All of creation is sacred. Everything that exists is a part of that sacred creation. All the parts are related and interdependent. No part is more and/or less important than any other part.*

The Principle of Humility goes hand-in-hand with the Right to Be. The Right to Be sets the stage, and the Principle of Humility instructs us about our attitude. This principle tells us that all of creation is sacred, and that no part is more and/or less than any other part. This means that Universal Flow does not "favor" any being or species, including humans. From this perspective, we are not innately more valuable or important than all the other beings. That means we are not the pinnacle of creation.

The Principle of Humility asks us to recognize the sacredness of all other beings, including the Earth and all its resources. It asks us to acknowledge the truth of our relationship and interdependence with everything that exists. In practice, it asks us to always grant the Right to Be to whoever or whatever is before us.

The practice of Humility is actually very practical. It balances our human tendency to extremism. It elevates our consciousness and enables us to look at situations more clearly. It helps us recognize that the needs of others are equally important to our own, and *more* important than our *wants*. This helps us prioritize. The Principle of Humility also helps us create relationships that work. It helps us remember to treat others with respect, because it reminds us to see and honor their inherent sacredness. True humility also helps us to be more aware of our limitations, which helps us manage our egos, and be in balance.

The practice of true humility is difficult for humans. Our egos and insecurities get in the way. We might resist it because we think we need to be special in order to feel secure, or be motivated to achieve. This is an illusion; it comes from our lack of realistic awareness of our own nature. The truth is that when we learn to practice true, functional humility we have a better sense of reality. This includes our role in the greater whole. This opens the door to greater joy.

Applying the Principle of Humility to Business

Here are some examples of how the Principle of Humility can benefit the business world:

- It helps us recognize the degree to which we are dependent upon others—our customers, suppliers, fellow employees, the community, and the Earth itself. When we are successful, it helps us realize how others have contributed to our success. It helps us acknowledge how others have cooperated to create our success, so we are motivated to give back in proportion to what we have received.

- It prevents us from going to extremes. This creates balance and harmony, which is very beneficial. One example is the huge discrepancy now between CEO pay and worker salaries, which is currently more than 400 times that of an hourly worker.

East: The Principle of Acceptance—

As we humans understand it: *Everything that exists is accepted as it is, unconditionally. There is no judgment or restriction.*

At the Universal level, everything that exists is accepted as it is, as a part sacred creation. Everything has the right to exist, as it is. There are no conditions, restrictions, or judgments as to its worthiness. When humans truly and unconditionally practice acceptance, this frees energy, and puts us in touch with Universal Flow.

As a guideline for human behavior, the Principle of Acceptance is about working with reality *as it is*, not as we want it to be. It is part of recognizing all others' Right to Be, and adjusting our attitude with true humility. Acceptance begins with an *assessment process*. One notes the similarities and differences between one's self and the other. Then, and only then, one takes the active step of accepting the reality of the other as the other is, *in toto*, unconditionally. This is true acceptance. Although it's a challenge for us to accept things that we fear or disapprove of, it is necessary. Whenever we refuse to accept something we block the flow of energy. When we practice acceptance, those blockages dissolve. This frees the energy of the Universe, making it available for us.

The Principle of Acceptance tells us that we must accept a

person or idea *as it is*, without becoming impatient with it. It teaches us to accept *what is*. And so, we learn patience, as well as the capacity to change, and to allow for change.

We must stress that Universal Acceptance is not synonymous with unquestioning approval. It does not mean that we give up our capacity for discernment. As with most things, moderation is the key to working with the Principle of Universal Acceptance. When we're in true alignment with this principle, we'll know when to compromise and when to be compassionate.

There is a great deal of domination and exploitation in the world today. Ironically, those who dominate or exploit others are often deeply plagued by questions of their own self-worth and "right to be." Much of this behavior is compensation for self-doubt. As the Dalai Lama has noted, self-hate and low self-esteem are pervasive in the West. Many of us are descended from immigrants or refugees who left their home countries due to poverty, starvation, or prejudice. The legacy of this history is that many of us grow up within a framework of perceived scarcity and persecution, rather than abundance and well-being. We fear that there is not enough, so we justify taking more than we need. Much of this behavior is unconscious and unexamined. We have developed elaborate justifications this behavior, and these habits are so ingrained that they are difficult to change.

The practice of acceptance can set us free of that self-induced turmoil. As we let go of energetic blockages such as prejudice, judgment, or righteousness, energy flows back to us. This energetic surge gives us strength and inspiration. We feel full of the desire to let go of the burden of negative energy patterns. When we learn to live in accordance with these Laws and Principles, we experience our own right to be honored and accepted.

Applying the Principle of Acceptance to Business

The Principle of Acceptance is very important for creating good partnerships. We're often tempted to enter into partnerships, without really understanding the true capacities of our partners (or the lack thereof). We get swept up in good feelings. We don't want to spoil the mood, so we tell ourselves that we'll be able to do something about problems if they crop up later. That seldom works, as you've probably experienced. The truth is, we must first accept *what is* before we can refine it. We must understand our similarities and differences, first. Then we can accept our partner as they are, in toto. Only when we have truly accepted each partner, including oneself, can we really benefit from the gifts and talents of everyone involved. Only then is it possible to address and compensate for frailties. This is applicable to equipment as well as people.

The Principle of Acceptance also applies to the deadlines we set. We often set them based on our ideals, rather than on a realistic assessment of what's possible. We can build appropriate easement into our schedules only when we have accepted what is.

Southeast: The Universal Law of Chaos

As we humans understand it: *Chaos is energy flowing in multiple directions at the same time. Chaotic energy will eventually resolve itself, without intervention. It will become directed, and lead to change.*

We use the term "chaos" to describe what we experience when energy seems to have no discernible shape or pattern. Chaos makes us fearful, but the actions we take out of our fear of chaos often make the experience worse. To further the irony, chaos is often the result of human action. The events surrounding September 11, 2001 are a prime example. It was a human-engineered event that engendered widespread chaos. Our fear response actually amplified it.

If humans learn to see and acknowledge their role in chaotic situations, it helps us to diminish our fear. We'll also be less fearful of chaos if we have a better understanding of its nature. Chaos is not energy that has *no* direction; it's energy that is flowing in multiple directions at the same time. It's *energy in search of direction*. The Universal Law of Chaos says that *chaotic energy will eventually resolve itself.* Chaos will become directed, and it *will eventually lead to change.* Put simply, chaos is change in process. We humans tend to resist change, so this is part of what makes chaos so uncomfortable for us. By accepting the inevitability of change and allowing it to proceed at its own natural pace, without applying unnecessary force in the hopes of achieving a premature resolution, we increase our capacity to cope in times of apparent chaos.

The Universal Law of Chaos is in the Southeast to remind us that we can work with this energy as a resource. This quadrant of the Circle is about rallying resources to bring about a vision. In essence, this is the place where chaos transitions into order. We can't effectively control, resist, or diminish chaotic energy. We can, however, *give it direction* to bring about positive change.

Applying the Law of Chaos to Business

- Recognize that a certain amount of chaos as inevitable. Anticipate that certain business events—even very positive events such as growth and success—will trigger a certain amount of chaos.
- Exercise prudence with respect to managing chaos. Ironically, we tend to create more chaos when we try to control things. Remember that chaos will resolve itself. We need to give it direction.
- We can create chaos by introducing too much change all at once. This is important in change management work. Moderate the amount of human-directed change in your business, to allow for positive benefits.
- Acknowledge that every human act has an effect on the energy field, and that the human being can be unpredictable. Recognize that some people in your organization may actually love chaotic energy, and will try to create chaos whenever they can.

Southeast: The Universal Law of Honor

As we humans understand it: *Energy is given direction through the acceptance of and respect for the survival needs of others.*

At the Universal level, the survival needs of all beings are allowed and included; they are all part of the Great Circle. In this way, those needs are honored. On the human plane, we abide by the Universal Law of Honor when we accept and respect the survival needs of others. We must also accept and respect their values, when these are based in survival needs.

All beings in existence communicate their survival needs and related values. Every being communicates differently, but the communication is there, to be heard, or observed. The leaves of a lemon tree turn yellow, communicating its need for nutrients. Another plant wilts, indicating its need for moisture. A wolf in search of its lost mate may howl at the moon. A nest full of baby birds chirp frantically to be fed. A cat purrs, expressing its pleasure. Weather is a great communicator: Dark, menacing storm clouds signal their need to burst forth with moisture. Humans communicate what they need and value in multiple ways: through signs, symbols, gestures, speech, and even clothing.

Humans generally engage with the Law of Honor through words. By declaring what we intend to honor, we give direction and focus to our actions: we direct energy. The more we express our intention to honor the needs and values of others, the more we align with the Universal Law of Honor, which helps put us in touch with Universal Flow. Written documents that show the power of words to direct energy include the Declaration of the Rights of Man and of the Citizen, the Declaration of Independence, the Emancipation Proclamation, and the Universal Declaration of Human Rights.

The Law of Honor is in the Southeast because this direction represents the transition between thought and action, between vision and manifestation. Here, we give direction to the flow of energy, so that we can manifest our ideas in the South.

Applying the Law of Honor to Business

We've gotten to a place in business today where it seems that honor is disappearing. Often, speed and profit-making are increasingly more important than value, worth, and quality. The loss of these things makes us less than we are, and less than we're capable of being.

We easily use the words, "I honor this," but what does that really mean? The Law of Honor asks us to really think about what we value. What, specifically, do we honor? What do we truly value? The Law of Honor asks us to create a set of written guidelines, reflecting the values and standards we wish to live by and run our business by. It's important that we write down the principles and values we intend to uphold, and the specific actions we will take in order to do that. It is here that we specify what we will do to respect the sacred beingness of others and the Earth. In this way, we lay the moral and ethical foundation for our business. This creates an energetic field that holds our commitments. This in turn becomes part of the flow of the business. Only then does Honor become something real, and not just a cliché.

- The Law of Honor asks that we create a code of ethics for ourselves, and our business. It's important to put these values down on paper.

- The Law of Honor asks us to describe the specific actions and behaviors that support those values. For example, if you say you want to honor both the property of others and of the business, what does that look like in action? Putting these things in writing will communicate to your employees what these values and standards are, and what they actually look like in the conduct of business.

- Use the Law of Honor to guide you in creating your business policies and procedures. Say, for example, you want to give preferential treatment to certain customers. You begin by stating that you value *all* your customers.

You then describe how you will demonstrate this. Once that is complete, you are ready to formulate a policy describing the process by which a customer can earn the privilege of preferential treatment.

South: The Universal Law of Altruism

As we humans understand it: *Energy is always flowing in the way that will create the greatest benefit for all, including itself. This is the Universal Law of Altruism.* It asks each being to *do that which works best for all concerned, including oneself.* When we do so, we align with Universal Flow. This creates a state of well-being, balance, and harmony that benefits us all.

After the Right to Be, the Law of Altruism is the most important. It says that Universal Energy always flows in such a way as to create the greatest benefit for all. Each and every being is enjoined to do the same. Whenever there is a question about to how to act, choose to do *that which works best for all concerned, including oneself.* This is the true meaning of altruism.

For humans, one of the biggest challenges to practicing the Law of Altruism is to really understand it. Presently, it's quite misunderstood. Some people mistakenly believe that altruism is synonymous with self-sacrifice, that it means we should put the welfare of others first, to the exclusion of our own well-being. This is an extremist view, and is not what altruism actually means. When we don't include ourselves in the equation, this often leads to undesirable by-products, like hidden anger or self-righteousness. For many, learning to consider oneself in the equation will be the biggest challenge.

Others will tend to reject altruism because they mistake it for unrealistic idealism. They consider it inconsistent with survival, which they believe requires self-interest at the cost of others. They are stuck in misunderstanding and shortsightedness. Under their misunderstanding is fear. They're fearful that in considering the needs of others, they will not get enough. They may also be worried that they will become overwhelmed by the needs of others.

They may feel inadequate to know what is best for all.

The Law of Altruism requires a deliberate and highly conscious practice. When we are called upon to decide how to act, we must undertake to learn *what actually will work best for all concerned, including ourselves.* We cannot just assume that we already know. It also asks us to be conscious of our tendency to extremism.

We can't practice the Law of Altruism in a naïve way. We must combine it with a good deal of social and political savvy in order to bring it to bear with real effect in the world. It would be helpful if we had many human examples of altruism to follow. Unfortunately, few human examples exist at this time. Jimmy Carter is one of the few people in the public eye who works at altruism. The Harlem Globe Trotters are also a good example in how they work as a team. We have examples of what happens when we don't align with the Law of Altruism. Recent corporate scandals are examples wherein we create problems for others and for ourselves. Ironically, these actions create consequences that reinforce our ideas about the world being an innately hostile place. This becomes the self-reinforcing trap that keeps us operating out of fear and narrow self-interest. To move the human race forward, the Law of Altruism must replace fear as a basis for our choices.

There are many examples of altruism in the natural world, and we can use them for guidance. We can see this at work in a wolf pack. We see it in the migration of birds. Geese, heron, and cranes all migrate in the "V" formation where the wiser, stronger, and more experienced birds take turns being in the lead position of the point bird. The leaders are responsible for cutting through the wind and air pressure, while the others in the flock get the benefit of drafting behind. If you observe birds re-aligning, you will see them rotating responsibility. When the bird in the point position has done its stint, it will move around to the end, which is the best position for catching the draft from the others. Another bird will take its turn as the lead. This teamwork benefits the entire flock.

Initially, we may find that working with the Law of Altruism feels strange and unfamiliar. However, when we turn to the Law of Altruism for guidance, we receive greater clarity. The Universe does not expect us to be "perfect." It is important to accept our human limitations, and do the best we can. Our efforts will align us with the larger, energetic flow of the Universe. When we make choices and decisions based on what works best for all concerned, including ourselves, we become part of the something larger than ourselves, the Great Circle, and our efforts align with the larger flow of Universal Energy. When we operate in accordance with the Law of Altruism we feel a sense of peace and harmony that is immeasurably satisfying.

Applying the Law of Altruism to Business

The most basic brick in the foundation of your business is your motivation for being in business in the first place. Today it appears that most business creation is motivated by financial gain, even greed. Many people make business and career choices based on their desire to make money. It may seem counterintuitive to many, but businesses that rest on a foundation of altruism have the best chance of success. If you are motivated to do what is best for all concerned, including yourself, the foundation of your business will be strong and sustainable. If, however, you are motivated primarily by profits, the foundation will be shaky. Here's why: At first glance, our current focus on self-interest looks very functional. What could be more effective to ensuring survival and success than looking out for oneself, exclusively? This taken-for-granted notion proves false in actuality. It's a law of nature that the more any being gets too focused on any one thing—even its own survival—the less easily it can change and adapt to its environment. The same is true for a business. Businesses need flexibility; they need to quickly adapt to market changes. The narrow focus that comes out of our linear pattern does not work in their favor.

Narrowness of focus is maladaptive because it restricts our field of vision. As our vision gets narrower and narrower, we see only an increasingly smaller aspect of reality. As our ability to see circumstances diminishes, so does our ability to adapt to change in those circumstances. In nature as in business, any creature that can't adapt to change has a shortened life span. They may seem to prevail in the short-term, but they do not endure. Enron, Montgomery Ward, and Firestone are good examples.

In today's business environment, businesses are required to be agile. That requires a more open and inclusive perspective than ever before. Businesses founded on the Law of Altruism will leave a lasting legacy. Altruistic motivations expand your capacity for vision. When you are able to consider what is best for all concerned, you can respond readily to the marketplace, and provide what the customer wants and needs. Use the Law of Altruism to:

- **Perform a periodic check on your motivation** - Is your motivation expansive and altruistic? If not, you maybe unnecessarily narrowing your focus, and thus your field of vision.

- **Check your hiring practices** – When you look at your hiring practices through the lens of altruism you may see that you may tend to hire only certain kinds of people. The Law of Altruism may help you to expand your horizons, so that you have a broader range of hiring options.

- **Guide all strategic business decisions** – The Law of Altruism asks you to consider what is best for all concerned with your business. This includes your customers, employees, and suppliers, as well as the owners and stockholders. It also includes the industry of which you are a part, the surrounding community, and the environment. This is a stretch from current practice, but it leads to long-term viability. A business that is focused narrowly on its own self-preservation will endanger its survival due to loss of flexibility, adaptability, and vision.

- **Evaluate your business** - When you evaluate your business looking through the lens of altruism, what does that tell you about the true state of your business? What does it tell you about how you are treating your customers, suppliers, and employees, the surrounding community, and any other stakeholders? Altruism is also the guidepost we use when we conduct our assessment and evaluation in the Western direction.

South: The Universal Law of Integrity

As we humans understand it: *Universal Energy supports the flow of ideals, morals, and values into movement and manifestation.*

The Law of Integrity completes the Law of Honor. In the Southeast we spoke of the importance of giving voice to what we honor. That act gives direction to energy. Our words set energy in motion. This is the meaning of the Law of Honor. Our actions must then follow through. We are in integrity when we take action based on what we Honor. When our actions match our words, then energy flows and that which we honor begins to manifest in the world. This is the meaning of the Law of Integrity. When our actions match our words, then we operate with integrity, and we have access to Universal support. When our actions don't match our words, we create "dis-connects." These contradictions block the flow of energy, so the momentum we created in the Southeast is stopped and energy scattered, which loops it back into chaos.

Applying the Law of Integrity to Business

In business, words are not enough. Ideas are not enough. The Law of Integrity helps us with making thoughts and ideas a physical reality. It helps us with commitment. The Law of Integrity helps a business stay in Universal Flow. Here are some of the ways in which businesses can practice the Law of Integrity:

- Make sure your business has systems in place to reinforce people acting in accordance with the code of ethics you created in the Southeast.

- One of the places where we commonly drop our integrity is in our relationship with customers. We may say that we value them, but frequently when we discover we can't meet customer expectations, we go out of integrity. The Law of Integrity says that you stay true to your word and your values. That may mean that you take a very straightforward approach to problems. You keep customers in the loop, and you get back to them. You keep communicating until the problem is solved.

- Leadership is responsible for exemplifying integrity. Those of us in leadership must walk our talk.

South: The Universal Law of Change

As we humans understand it: *Energy is always in motion, so everything is always in the process of change.*

As we have said, energy moves constantly throughout the universe. Therefore, *things will change.* Change is inevitable. This is the nature of the universe.

"Change" is the word we use to describe energy that has a clear direction; we can see where it's heading. In general, human beings try to hold on to the status quo, as it makes us feel comfortable. This is unrealistic, because change is the nature of the Universe. So, the best option we have is to learn to *accept and cooperate with the flow of change that is already in motion.* When we do this, we will experience being supported by the Universe.

This is a major shift for most of us. We want to control and force things to occur the way we want them, disregarding the way energy is flowing of its own accord. We do this out of insecurity. Ultimately, this is a much lonelier journey, since it puts us at odds with the universe. Ironically, we are actually *more* in control when we cooperate with the flow of change rather than work against it. The Law of Change is such a powerful force, that it will ultimately prevail. The more willing we are to surrender to the flow of change, the more supported we will feel, and *the more likely we are to have some influence over the direction of the change.* Counter-intuitive though it may seem, the more we cooperate (and give up absolute control), the more likely we are to feel empowered, and to experience a positive outcome.

Applying the Law of Change to Business

How, specifically, can we apply this understanding of the Laws of Change and Chaos to managing a business? People in business must work with change, with the unexpected, and at moments, with chaos. There are ways that a business can prepare for change and chaos, such that we have the ability to recover quickly with the least amount of damage to our business. Not only must we learn to anticipate change and chaos, but we must also learn to respond accordingly. Here are some suggestions:

- Set your attitude and expectations. Since energy is in constant motion, use this understanding to accept the inevitability of change and even chaos. Anticipate their occurrence. Resist enforcing status quo as the norm. Fighting change is a losing battle, costly both in terms of our resources and our peace of mind. Build a certain amount of easement into business plans so that you are prepared for change from the very start.

- Recognize the types of events that commonly trigger change and chaos. Expect that success is likely to create change, and even amplify it into chaotic energy. Recognize that a major growth spurt will also tend to generate some chaos. We may want steady, pain-free, consistent growth to be the norm, but this is unlikely. A realistic attitude will help prevent the business from being blindsided by the consequences of rapid growth or, alternatively, the slower periods of the cycle.

- Learn to recognize a shift in energy patterns, so that you can invoke your contingency plans when change begins to occur. This will help prevent the change from turning into total chaos. If you experience a chaotic energy pattern, anticipate what changes it will lead to and prepare for them.

- Prepare for the inevitable. In particular, anticipate and plan for those energy patterns that are most likely to affect your business. Tune in to your immediate environment, your community, and your people. By doing so you'll be much more attuned to the kinds of changes that are likely to occur. For example, anticipate and plan for the natural disasters that are likely in your immediate environment. Suppose your business is located in a potential flood zone in Minnesota. What do you do when Minnesota floods? Notice also how the economy goes through periodic cycles of ups and downs in our economic flow. Anticipate economic downturns, and build contingencies into your business plan. Describe what, specifically, you're going to do when these anticipated changes or chaos occurs.

- Involve the people in your organization in both anticipating and planning for change. If possible, run simulations—like fire drills—so people in the organization can practice responding in a timely fashion, and you can learn about how effective your response plan is.

- Engage with the Law of Altruism, acknowledging that the energy of the universe is flowing in the direction that works best for all concerned. Then look at how you can cooperate with that flow of energy.

- Refrain from introducing too much human-directed change into your life and/or your business in a short period of time. This is likely to trigger a sense of chaos. Work at moderation.

In sum, both change and chaos are inevitable. If business can develop a healthier attitude about this by building change into their business plans from the very beginning, they would also be developing their ability to work with change functionally. Then you have a business that has tremendous flexibility, tremendous adaptability, and the benefit of longevity. (Also, see the Universal Law of Chaos.)

Southwest: The Principle of Compassion

As we humans understand: *Universal flow allows the processes of all individuals to ensue, without interference.*

The Principle of Compassion has, for a long time, been a subject of debate and intellectual conversation. That is because compassion is complex; there is the universal perspective and the human perspective.

At the level of Universal Flow, compassion is non-interference. The universal perspective says that all beings have rights. These include the Right to Be and the rights to equitable exchange, unconditional love, truth, balance, acceptance, and co-operation, as well as the right to grow and change. All beings also have the right to make mistakes in the process of aligning with Universal Flow. Universal Compassion, expressed through non-interference, comes into play when an individual is struggling with these rights and processes. The Universe allows those struggles to ensue, without interference because it is through these labors that we learn the life lessons necessary for our sustained survival. The original Star Trek series recognized this Universal Principle of Compassion; it's what they referred to as the "Prime Directive".

At the Universal level, non-interference works. On the human plane, however, inaction is not always benign. Sometimes we need to make adjustments to make things work better. As empathic beings, we feel for each other. We know many of us are caught up in human-created systems or cultures that are not fair or just. In most cases, these systems do not support the range of principles that are important for a fulfilling existence. They do not support the Right to Be, equitable exchange, unconditional love, universal truth, balance, non-interference, acceptance and co-operation. We want to help, and so we humans re-defined "compassion" to include being kind, considerate, empathetic, and caring. We expanded the meaning of compassion to include getting involved, helping others, and working toward making life conditions more just and fair. This includes helping someone when they are down on their luck, or funding charities to help disaster victims.

Both definitions of compassion are going on within us, which is why it's such a hotly contested ideal. Living in accordance with the Principle of Compassion is about balancing the universal/divine perspective and the human. The Principle of Compassion asks us to be present to the situation in the moment. Sometimes we need to get out of the way (non-interference), and sometimes we need to get involved. The key is in knowing which is most appropriate to the situation.

Because of our empathic tendencies, we can get swept up in the energy of the situation. We can become confused by others' have strong opinions about what compassion should look like. The Principle of Compassion reminds us to find our own truth, and act accordingly. In the midst of these situations, the Circle can help you find clarity. It can help you balance the universal and human perspectives. (For more on this, please see the *Compassion Help Circle* in the Appendix.)

Applying the Principle of Compassion in Business

Perhaps it will surprise you to learn that compassion has a place in business. It does. It comes into play when you need to rectify imbalances. Imbalances are injurious to your business. And, *both types of compassion are necessary* to running a business. That's the only way you'll create balance. Typical imbalances that need rectification through the application of the Principle of Compassion include the following:

- Employees are being "consumed" due to excessive hours, or not being paid a living wage.

- The environment is being polluted or ruined, and resources irrevocably depleted because of business practices.

- The business is ignoring its social responsibility to its customers, or the community.

- The business has acquired a surplus of profit or wisdom, which it hoards, rather than shares.

West: The Universal Law of Transition

As we humans understand it: *Naturally occurring transitions happen in the way that is best for all concerned.*

We use the word "transition" to describe a specific kind of energetic flow. A transition is the process of movement from one energetic state to another. Since change is constant, so is transition.

Naturally occurring transitions happen in the way that is best for all concerned (i.e., they happen in accordance with the Universal Law of Altruism). That doesn't mean we humans will necessarily feel comfortable when we are experiencing a transition. We tend to perceive any transition as bigger than it is; we fear that it will have more impact on us than it actually will. Out of this insecurity, we'll try to control a transition rather than just exercising some direction or letting it go and following the stream of energy. This is our extremist tendency getting in the way of a naturally occurring phenomenon. If we allow it to guide us instead of trying to dominate it, we'll see that a natural transition aligns with that which is best for all concerned.

Applying the Law of Transition to Business

Transitions are happening all the time in business, though they may not call attention to themselves. The Law of Transition tells us to:

- Anticipate the most obvious causes of transitions across the business and within individual departments. That way, they do not come as a surprise. For example, your R&D and Sales & Marketing departments should always be actively anticipating, and welcoming, new customer/market needs and demands. Production should anticipate changes in resources and suppliers.

- Acknowledge transitions when they occur, such as the departure of a Management Team member.

- Cooperate with these natural transitions when they occur. Remember, they are happening in accordance with the Law of Altruism, so we should not interfere with them, try to control them, or resist them.

- When you undertake a change, moderate the speed and depth of the change so that transitions are not as stressful or become chaotic.

- Set up logistics to support a smooth transition. For example, you may want to create a temporary counseling center when the business undergoes a major transition.

Northwest: The Principle of Equitable Exchange

As we humans understand it: *At the level of Universal Flow, everything operates in the basis of equitable exchange. This is the Great Circle. When one being receives (or takes) something from another being, there must be a mutually beneficial return in order for Universal support and flow to continue.*

The way of the universe is to flow toward balance. Balance is *not a static state*; it's a *process*. In other words, the Universe is always *in the process of creating* greater balance and harmony. The process that creates this balance is equitable exchange.

The Principle of Equitable Exchange is embedded in all natural processes. All natural processes are cycles in which there is a process of mutually beneficial exchange, a process of receiving and giving back in equal measure. We enter into this great circle of exchange when we draw our first breath. Our breath is a crucial part of a circle: We breathe in oxygen, and breathe out carbon dioxide. Plants complete the cycle: They respire by "breathing in" carbon dioxide and "breathing out" oxygen. The entire circle is equitable and mutually beneficial for all concerned.

The most important thing for humans to understand about this particular principle is that *we have the responsibility to participate in that balancing process.* In particular, it is important for us to keep things in balance in our relationships with other beings, including the Earth. The essential meaning of this principle is that when we receive (or take) something from another being, we must return that offering in a way that is equitable to the recipient.[15] If we do not, the Universe will go about creating balance in its own way. This may or may not be to our benefit.

As humans, we engage in transactions all the time. The intention behind this principle is to encourage humans to bring more consciousness into those transactions, so that we participate in the balancing process and don't succumb to extraction or exploitation. The principle of Equitable Exchange helps us consciously acknowledge the truly interdependent nature of our existence. It helps us shift from a consumptive, dominating mindset (which has become so embedded in our way of life that we embody it consistently and unconsciously), to one of mutuality.

The Principle of Equitable Exchange asks us to give back something that is truly of equivalent value as experienced by the other. That is a very different than just giving back whatever we happen to have, or whatever *we* experience as valuable. Like the Law of Altruism, this principle asks us to discover *what the other being actually needs and values.* It also poses another important set of questions: What does an equitable exchange with the Earth look like? Given where we are now, how do we repay the Earth for all that we have taken from her?

The Principle of Equitable Exchange also applies to the cycle of our lives. When we come into life we receive a great deal;

hopefully, we are supported and nurtured as we are supposed to be. Then, as we go through life we have a responsibility to give back for all that we have received from nature, from the earth, from all those who have participated in our lives. This mutual exchange of energy keeps the Great Wheel turning, and when we participate in it we experience a great sense of appropriateness, harmony, fulfillment, and joy.

In sum, all beings share in the process of the Universe working in harmony and balance. We humans should consider each and every transaction in light of the Principle of Equitable Exchange in order to remain a viable, connected part of the Universe.

Applying the Principle of Equitable Exchange to Business

Business is, by definition, a process of exchange: goods and services are being exchanged for money, and vice versa. The Principle of Equitable Exchange says that these transactions are most satisfying when they are *equitable* and *mutually beneficial to all parties involved,* on both the physical and energetic planes.

- Equitable exchange should be the goal of all business transactions. This is lost today.

- Businesses that look to create mutual benefit on both levels create strong relationships. This is key to the long-term success of a business.

- The process of equitable exchange yields abundant by-products. People feel they are being treated fairly. This creates comfort, and greater opportunity for further exchange.

- If you create a constant cycle of equitable exchange, then the energetic flow never stops. This creates relationships permeated with trust and safety, loyalty, consistency, and prosperity.

- The practice of equitable exchange enhances our ability to manifest. This creates greater prosperity for all involved.

- The ongoing practice of equitable exchange helps create sustainability for our businesses and our species on this planet.

North: The Universal Law of Transformation

As we humans understand it: *All things go through a transformation during their existence. All naturally occurring transformations happen in accordance with the Universal Law of Altruism—to the greater benefit of all.*

"Transformation" is the word we use to describe the process of going from one kind of energetic state to another kind. *All things go through a transformation during their existence.* This is inevitable. Everything that is starts as one thing, and ends as something else. For example, a baby becomes an adult. This is an obvious transformation. Other transformations are more internal and subtle.

People go through transformations all the time, often without realizing it. Whenever we finish a cycle, we've just finished a major transformational pattern, so we're no longer the same. However, we are culturally conditioned not to deal with transformations in a highly conscious way. We don't realize that with any transformation comes a *whole new set of energetic patterns*. Because we don't acknowledge transformations, we don't work with them effectively. When we haven't anticipated and planned for them, they can overwhelm us.

Energy flows, and so natural transitions and transformations happen of their own accord, in the way that is best for all concerned. We have difficulty trusting these natural processes. We want to control them because we believe that's they only way to guarantee our interests will be supported. *Human beings enhance their experience of Universal Flow when they recognize and accept naturally occurring transformations, rather than resisting or interfering with them.* If we try to work against these universal laws and principles, the universe will look and feel more hostile to us. If, however, we can learn to accept these natural transformations, we'll have an easier time making sense of our experience and dealing with it effectively. Acceptance gives us greater clarity and enhances our ability to plan. By working consciously with the transformations that occur in our lives, we improve our ability to utilize the energy that is available at these times. This enables us to bring greater fruition and maturity into the results.

Applying the Law of Transformation to Business

The Law of Transformation applies to anything and everything that exists, including a business. Companies go through more minor transformations all the time without necessarily recognizing them or dealing with them most effectively. Here are some guidelines for working with the Law of Transformation:

- Your business will naturally go through at least one transformation as part of its existence. Anticipate this point of natural transformation. Plan for it, acknowledge it when it arrives, accept it, anticipate the consequences, and trust the process (rather than resisting it).

- Transformation in the business world takes many forms. Minor transformations include changes in policies, management, or systems. Major transformations include the demise of a product line, restructuring, or a merger with another company.

- If you find yourself trying to keep your business just the same as it always has been, you're trying to resist a transformation. By not allowing that flow to happen, you're fighting a Universal Law. This takes your business out of Universal Flow. Take, for example, when a small neighborhood store that sees its business being taken over by a mega-store. Resisting the transformation is likely to be futile; stepping back and looking for how we might change is fertile ground. The mega-store may not able to provide personal service. A small operation can. There is a golden opportunity for the small business to undergo a transformation: to specialize in personal service. This would enable the neighborhood store to peacefully, and profitably, coexist with the larger store.

- Humans can instigate transformations. For example, a company may decide it needs to change its focus, intention, by-laws, management, etc. This could result in minor, or major transformations. For example, if a company decided to make the environment and worker needs a higher priority, this would constitute a major transformation.

- If you need or desire to lead your business through a transformation, you will trigger fewer complications if you break the transformation into a series of transitions or incremental changes. We in the business world are often engaged with actively trying to "transform" our businesses, without understanding fully the nature of transformation. We often want to change everything all at once, but humans have a tendency become stressed and emotional during transformations. Moving too quickly increases the sense of instability. A transformation is actually comprised of many transitions. So, if you want to take your business through a transformation comfortably, do so in a step-by-step manner, by making incremental changes. An incremental approach will create greater stability throughout the process. By going slower, you will get to your goal faster. Otherwise, you risk creating chaos, and not transformation.

North: The Universal Law of Transmutation

As we humans understand it: *Sometimes, in nature, change is so profound that it results in a whole new energetic being. This is transmutation.*

A transmutation happens when an individuated energy, that has its own identity, changes or evolves into a whole new energetic existence. The new existence is totally changed in form, chemical make-up (not always at level of DNA), and constructive (i.e., base root, energetic) elements. The old being is no longer in existence; a new individuation has formed. In the process of transmutation the energetic stream is not lost, as the being recalls were it has come from.

An example of transmutation in nature is the journey of a caterpillar into a chrysalis, and its emergence as a butterfly. Conception, birth, and death are also transmutation processes.

Humans enhance their experience of flow when they anticipate and accept appropriate transmutations. Even when they are very positive, transmutations can be stressful to the human psyche. They trigger our insecurity. For that reason, we may be tempted to downplay them. In actuality, we need to openly acknowledge them, and work with the Principle of Acceptance.

Applying the Law of Transmutation to Business

Although not the daily norm, transmutations are a fact of life. They will occur in the life cycle of a business. For example, giving birth to a business is a transmutive process. You are taking an idea, a thought form, and manifesting it in physical reality; that is a transmutation.

We need to work on accepting these transmutations when they are necessary as part of a business's life cycle. The demise of anything or anyone is a natural transmutation that we have a difficult time with. Anticipate that your people, resources, or even business may die. Plan for it and educate your workforce as you go. If and when the time comes, acknowledge the situation and practice the Principle of Acceptance.

Any transmutation, whether in our personal lives or in business, must be well-considered because it is a very profound change. Once started, there is no going back; you can only go forward until the transmutation process is complete. It is something to be avoided except when necessary. If you decide you must go through a transmutation process, do so with care. Engaging people on the outside, who can monitor the process, is extremely beneficial to all involved.

Ironically, we can bring about transmutations when they're not necessary. For example, an entrepreneur might be a "one-man" show. He or she might not train others to do what the business requires. By making the business overly dependent, h/she is forcing the business to shut down because it is impossible for anyone to do it all.

In addition, we can try to force transmutations to occur. When we believe that large system change is necessary, we can be extremists. For example, some take the position that we must shut down the entire capitalist system in order to resolve its inequities. They want to replace it with something else—without necessarily defining what that next stage is. It's true that the industrial world has forgotten the environment for most of several millennia. Now, that is catching up to us. If we make a radical shift, and remove our foundation of capitalism in its entirety, we will have a cultural breakdown where nothing works. A better strategy is to work on bridging from here to where we need to go. That is best done in smaller steps. If we create these bridges, we can help transition, and then transform the present system to its next evolutionary form. (This will be discussed in more detail in the final chapter.)

Northeast: The Universal Law of Cooperation

As we humans understand it: *Everything in the Universe is related, interconnected, and interdependent. Therefore, survival is enhanced through cooperation. The resulting movement of energy benefits all parties involved.*

Universal Energy flows in the direction of Altruism, supporting the existence and ongoing evolution of all. Individual energetic streams within Universal Flow stream together in harmonious patterns in order to fulfill the potential of the whole; they never obstruct, force, or subdue each other. Each individual being is allowed to fulfill their potential as well. This process is cooperation. Cooperation moves energy, which contributes to the flow of Universal Energy. Cooperation is the desired goal of Universal Flow because that creates more balance and harmony.

We align with this Law when we engage with others in an *agreed-upon process, in a way that is mutually beneficial for all concerned, and that results in some form of movement.* When humans interact in this way, we are able to help each other realize our individual destinies. This is likely to enhance our experience of Universal Flow.

Our culture often fails to teach the importance of cooperation, except in team sports. Many species—including humans—had to learn to cooperate to survive. In fact, our human vessels are made up of multiple parts that require cooperation (e.g., brain, heart, immunity system, etc.). Our species is now being presented with a major lesson involving this process. At this point in our history, our very survival depends upon our learning the lesson of how to bring about peaceful co-existence on earth. The Universal Law of Cooperation can help foster our ability to do this.

Applying the Law of Cooperation to Business

There is actually a great deal of cooperation involved in the conduct of business—we just tend not to recognize it or emphasize it. For example, the relationship between producer and customer is highly cooperative. Without each other, products would sit on the shelves or in the warehouse or customers would go without. We should always seek to make sure that our relationship with customers is an alliance that is mutually beneficial, not destructive. Collaborations and partnerships need to be collaborative, or they become counter-productive. These are many excellent opportunities in business for applying the Law of Cooperation to help support each party's individual destiny. Here are some suggestions:

- The conduct of business creates an energetic flow, which takes place within the larger flow of the community in which it's embedded. Ideally, these two flows will support each other, and flow together harmoniously. To foster this, businesses can work cooperatively with the communities of which they are a part. Both parties can strive to mutually support each other's goals. All parties are benefited in this way.

- Look to create alliances. Many of our business relationships are based on domination. Alliances, however, are deliberately and consciously created relationships, based in cooperation. In an alliance, no party seeks to dominate the other; the parties are equal, and the explicit goal is mutual benefit. An important fact about an alliance is that it is *not* necessary to love or even like the other party, or to agree with them philosophically. The only thing necessary is that the relationship be equitable and mutually beneficial, through coöperation.

- Think of your human resources as a cooperative alliance, with all the different talents creating mutual benefit. Avoid power games. They are based in dominance, and are counterproductive.

- Look to create an alliance with your technology. Think of it as a sacred tool, and treat it accordingly. (More on this in Volume 2.)

- Lawsuits against corporations are signs that the Law of Cooperation may have been broken. Usually, there has been some type of abuse of the rights or trust of the consumer.

Northeast: The Principle of Releasing and Letting Go

As we humans understand it: *At the Universal level, there is always movement. Energies make contact with one another, and support each other for as long as that exchange is mutually beneficial. When the exchange is complete, each is released. In the process of that dance, anything that hinders the ongoing flow of energy is also released. This process benefits the Greater Whole.*

In every exchange, no matter how minute, there is a releasing and letting go process. Releasing is part of the natural process of energetic movement from one state of being to another. Any undue hindrance of this process creates static, and will not last. It will be released and let go of in due time by the Universe. A consistent, regular flow, without hindrance, is easier and more harmonious for sentient creatures, such as ourselves.

Some natural releasing processes are easy and comfortable, whereas others can be aggressive and painful, and even destructive, particularly when there are hindrances to the process. The releasing of pressure through volcanic action is an example of the latter. Nature provides a stunning example of a cooperative, balanced, and harmonious releasing process. It is the circulatory system found in more evolved animals. A healthy heart uses constant, regular pulses and beats to transport a great deal of blood through a body. Various organs are constantly releasing nutrients, fresh cells, salts, hormones, and oxygen into the bloodstream. There, they are carried to where they are needed, and released. In exchange, the blood receives various toxic, waste products, which are transported and ultimately released and let go of (disposed of) by the body.

In human terms, the Principle of Releasing and Letting Go says that we must allow energy to flow; we cannot hold or impede the flow of energy merely to suit our wants or desires, as this creates static. Nor should we attempt to control some form of energetic flow that is not ours naturally, if doing so would be destructive to that energy. Slavery is a most egregious example. Sometimes, however, the releasing process needs restrictions and boundaries, for the good of the Whole. If we determine that we must hold or restrict any form of energy, we must do so very consciously, and only after carefully ascertaining that there is clear benefit to all concerned. This is particularly relevant to our interactions with the environment.

The Principle of Releasing and Letting Go is not easy for us humans because of our emotional investments. We get emotionally attached to things (people, behaviors, or ideas). We fear letting go, so we often hold on to the detriment, even possible destruction of the very thing we love. Sometimes, we have difficulty releasing things even if they are harmful to us. We would rather not face the unknown. It may take a great deal of personal pain before we are sufficiently motivated to let go.

For humans, releasing that which no longer works frees blocked energy, which opens the door to Universal Flow. We must continuously practice the art of releasing, if we want to stay in the flow of Universal Energy, and survive the experience. This principle is in the Northeast direction because it asks us to check and make sure that we have truly released and let go of anything that doesn't work, to avoid carrying it over to the next cycle.

Applying the Principle of Releasing & Letting Go to Business

This principle reminds us that we must be willing to let go of products, people, or strategies that no longer serve the needs of the business, or our customers. This can be quite difficult, as we may have made financial and/or emotional investments in them. However, letting go appropriately frees energy, which puts the business back in Universal Flow. Furthermore, it does the same for those things or people we release; they are actually freed to flow in a way that is more appropriate for them.

Center: The Law of Evolution

As we humans understand it: *Everything in the Universe is always in the process of change. Everything in the universe is entitled to experience the full measure of its existence. Everything is allowed—through non-interference—to learn, grow and change, in its own unique way, for its continued survival and sustainability, and for that of the Whole.*

The Universal Law of Evolution is supportive of everything, and everything's unique process. It saturates and permeates everything that exists, literally. This includes stars, planets, the air, plants, creatures, things, concepts, institutions, organizations, occupations, and systems of thought, and even business itself. The Law of Evolution is the culmination of all the other laws and principles we have been discussing.

To participate in the Law of Evolution we must allow ourselves as well as all others (such as our partners, co-workers, children, our business, and the community and environment) to each experience their unique journey and process. Equally important to experiencing the process is the task of working with the material from that experience. For us, this means wholeheartedly participating in some difficult periods of struggle, and working with the life lessons that emerge. Sometimes it means witnessing others as they grapple with important life passages, refraining from judging them or trying to control the outcome.

In order to work with Universal Energy and all its benefits, we humans have to engage with this law, but it is tempting to ignore what the Law of Evolution requires. It's more comfortable to stay in status quo. Doing so, however, creates stagnation, which can sabotage your business and stunt the growth of everybody and everything involved. Whether we choose to consciously engage with it or not, the Law of Evolution will definitely work on us, because we are a part of creation.

Change is an essential part of evolution. Because change tends to trigger our insecurity, we often have difficulty allowing and supporting evolutionary journeys—even our own. The use of the appropriate blueprint can help us with our resistance. The linear pattern does not facilitate evolution, but evolution is intrinsic to the Circle. As an example, the Circle blueprint naturally and easily supports us to conduct a review at the end of each day, week, month, or year (e.g., at the end of a cycle), where we reflect upon what went on, and what we have learned. When learning is ongoing and continuously supported in this way, it's much less threatening than when if comes at us all at once. Practices such as these enhance our evolutionary process so that it flows harmoniously.

Applying the Law of Evolution to Business

This law applies to the business itself, to the workers in the business, and to all the products and/or services in the business. It applies to everything involved. They all must be supported in their evolutionary journeys. Here are some of the ways to enact the Law of Evolution in business:

- The by-laws of every business should contain a statement in support of the Law of Evolution.

- Build evolutionary practices into your business's policies and practices. After-action reviews are especially beneficial. These are often conducted by the U.S. Army as an excellent way of inviting evolution into the way they work.

The Choice Before Us

Humans in all cultures have been studying and accumulating this wisdom for centuries, in order to learn how to be in greater harmony within ourselves and with all that exists. This wisdom exists because it was essential to our survival.

When all peoples around the world were much more primitive, we were much more keenly aware of the need to be in balance. When we weren't, the effect was immediate and potentially fatal. Overusing water, or other resources, could mean death, not just to the individual, but also to the entire group. Today, in modern life, we are removed from the effects of our actions. There is a lot of cushioning that prevents our experiencing the repercussions of our choices. In effect, we don't receive much-needed feedback. Thus, our guidance system is off: we have the illusion that our actions have no effect. In fact, what we know as "progress" can also be interpreted as movement away from the clear understanding of how to live in a balanced way. It appears that we've suppressed our wisdom in favor of ideas and beliefs that support our more self-centered habits. The Circle, in conjunction with these Universal Laws and Principles, can teach us how to live and peacefully co-exist with all that is.

We have the opportunity, now, to choose a different path. One of the fundamental premises of this book is that a business will be most successful, sustainable, and rewarding when it's conducted in a manner that is congruent with the laws and principles that govern the universe. Every business should have a written code of morals and ethics. These laws, principles, and the rights we will describe in the next chapter, are an excellent foundation for that moral code. This will start to bring the business into alignment with Universal Flow, and thus provide it with a tremendous source of energetic support. The continuous practice and reinforcement of that code will yield tremendous byproducts: it will create a strong and nourishing foundation for the business itself, and the people involved with the business will feel affirmed and invigorated. Loyalty, another valuable resource, will be fostered.

Aligning with these laws and principles brings us great rewards, but we must also acknowledge that it will not always be easy or comfortable. These laws and principles do not promote human dominance; they support the universe as a whole. Our deepest fears and insecurities will get triggered. The Law of Altruism will challenge us, because it's quite difficult for us to look at the big picture, and to put in the effort to understand things from another's perspective. Not only must we learn to do this with other humans, but we must also include the environment, the animals and plants, and everything else involved. We'll want to opt out of consciousness. We will always be tempted to stop. We'll want to say, "I was altruistic when I set up the business, so now I don't have to be." Not so. It comes down to commitment.

We must accept that, as humans, we're never going to reach perfection. We fall out of balance, and we weave in and out of alignment. That is our nature. The path may be difficult—but it's not *too* difficult. And the results are extremely fulfilling, commensurate with our efforts. Living in accordance of these laws and principles sets energy free. Instead of creating energy blockages that can last for generations, setting the energy free can release us from their burdens.

Everything works best when we align with these Laws and Principles and build them into our decision-making. This puts us in Universal Flow and gives us access to creative life force energy. All beings, including our businesses, are nurtured by this energy. Ultimately, we are assisted in our evolutionary process, inclusive of finding good, sustainable solutions to the challenges facing us in today's world.

Chapter Six
The Sacred Circle as a Way of Life:
A Blueprint for Peaceful Co-Existence

We are beginning to experience the limitations of our worldview in some very major ways. Our way of life no longer appears to be sustainable. But what can we do? How do we change? And, can we do it fast enough? Fortunately, we are not the first human beings to have arrived at a crossroads such as this. Others have been here before us. There is a story that explains how these earlier people came to recognize and develop a philosophy that sustained them. We may not have written records to tell us exactly how this philosophy originated, but there is an oral history. This is the story it tells.

A Gift from the Indigenous: The Rights of All Beings

Centuries ago, people lived differently than we do now. Indigenous people did not have the many layers of comfort and protection that cushions us today (and perhaps clouds our vision as well). Rather, indigenous peoples were dependent upon their immediate environment: the land upon which they lived, and the natural resources of that land. But, being human, they didn't learn to appreciate the extent of their dependency until it was almost too late. Like many of us today, they were focused on their own survival, and that of their immediate tribe. They had no regard to the larger ecosystem of which they were a part. They were nomadic. Wherever they set up camp they enjoyed the bounty that the forests, meadows, streams, lakes, rivers, and shorelines had to offer. When the season turned and resources were exhausted, they moved on to another location that offered fresh resources.

This scavenging lifestyle worked for many generations. In time, however, something happened. The people would return to places that had once been plentiful, only to find the resources decimated. They began to see that some of species they depended upon were diminishing. Some species even began to die out. The species that were disappearing first, were those that were most valued, those most often hunted or harvested.

In response, of course, human beings tried the easiest route. They tried to get what they needed from other human beings who were not from their tribe or nation. In essence, they were engaged in competition for land and natural resources. Quite often, this would lead to animosity and the animosity would lead to warring. If another group happened to be in a territory that had good resources, they raided or warred with that group so as to take over their resources or territory.

These early indigenous people didn't go to war for the reasons we modern people often do. Their reasons for going to war were elementary, not ideological. They made war because they needed food and territory. These wars were fierce. They attacked each other's villages, and set fire to the enemy's homes. In the process, the enemy tribe's supplies were often burned, and many women and children were killed. The warring escalated and spread, as wars do. So it came to pass that when a victorious war party returned home from a raid on another village—which they had destroyed—they found that their own village had been destroyed as well. They now had nothing to come home to.

These early people were not operating with the same intellectual consciousness that modern humans have; their sense of the world was rooted in body and emotion. Yet, they began to realize that these wars had no "winners." This strategy of annihilation wasn't functional, because raids—even if "successful"—would never achieve the purpose for which they had gone to war in the first place. Food was actually getting scarcer. They saw, too, that their numbers were dwindling. Many were dying in battle. Many of their women and children were being killed in enemy raids, which meant they couldn't replenish their lost numbers. War caused a depletion of human beings on both sides. These deaths diminished the populace at a time when human beings were scarce, and people were heavily dependent upon each other to perform necessary life tasks.

They began to understand that what was necessary for survival, was for humans to act with more moderation. They began to explore options. At first, they put in place some strategies to try to make warring more functional. They tried to respect each other's home territory by keeping the wars on separate battlegrounds, away from their homes. Another strategy was for each side to pick a single champion (or team), and only they would fight to the death. These strategies did not suffice, however, because that is the nature of war: it is chaotic energy, and it cannot be contained. The remaining human beings were in trouble. Their resources were depleted. They began to starve.

And so, out of this calamity, there arose a quest to find a way of being that could sustain people over the long term. How was it, they asked, that nature had sustained all the resources: creatures, trees, plants, land and water, before the arrival of humans? How did these beings all coexist without overrunning or killing each other off? What secrets did nature know that humans needed to learn, so they too, might survive?

Desperate, they turned to nature as a teacher. They asked to understand how it was that nature sustained so many species. They asked to be taught, and so began the long and arduous task of learning how they might live in harmony with the rest of existence, so that they might survive. They became true naturalists, studying the ways of the natural world.

And nature began to teach them. It began with a dawning

realization. In the wake of the carnage, the pillaged and burned-out homes, and the depleted supplies, they began to see that, by their own actions, they were killing themselves. As they looked deeply into the phenomena around them, they began to see a connection between how they lived, and how other beings lived. They began to see how everything in nature works in balance, and they began to see how their own out-of-balance actions had brought about their own near-destruction.

Gradually, they came to realize that their continued existence was bound to the continued existence of all other beings. This included their enemies. They came upon a simple, profound truth: The only way they were going to survive was to confer upon others the same right to existence to which they felt entitled. They must give others the *Right to Be*. Specifically, this meant they must allow their enemies to peacefully co-exist with them. This also meant they must allow the plants and creatures to peacefully co-exist. They must allow the females of enemy tribes to give birth and allow those babies to live and grow and mature in accordance with the natural order.

And so, little by little, a vision of the world and its relationship to the Universe began to emerge. This vision has been called the Sacred Circle of Life. From this vision comes the understanding that everything is made up of the same vital substance; everything is connected and related. The universe is a great chain of relationships linking all beings together in one great family. Out of that vision, a code for living in peaceful coexistence with all began to take wing. We call this the Rights of All Beings. The code states that we must honor and respect the right of all other beings to live their lives in accordance with their nature, without judgment, interference, or domination. Our survival depends upon our granting this right to all others; no other way of being ensures our own survival. In giving all others the Right to Be, we also give it to ourselves; it was, and is, a great Circle.

This ancient wisdom comes forward to help us re-learn how we might avoid self-destruction. Expressed as a Circle, these rights are as follows:

The Rights of All Beings

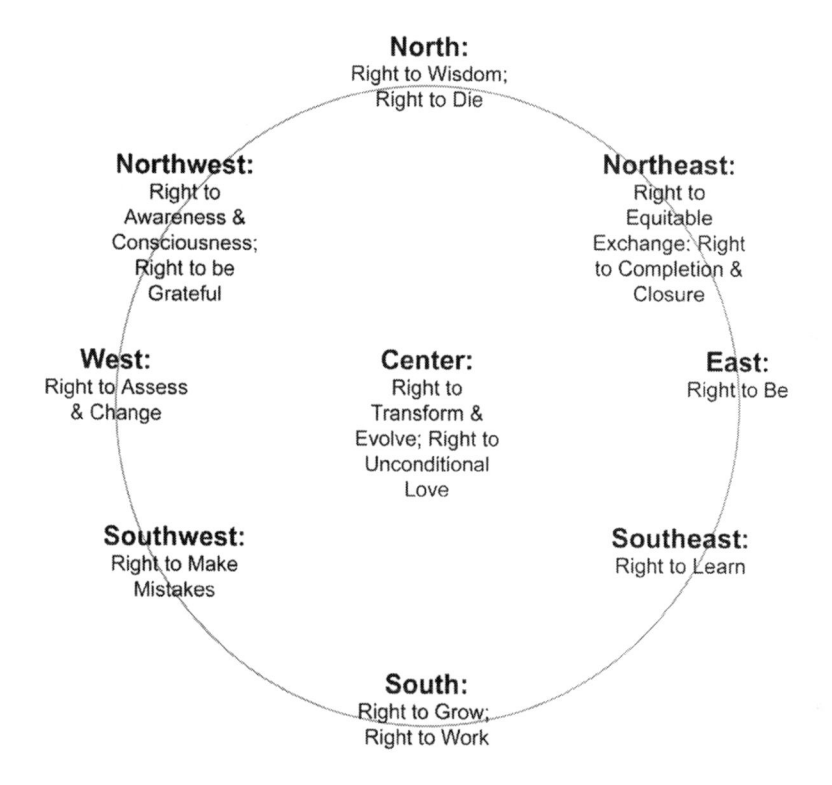

North:
Right to Wisdom;
Right to Die

Northwest:
Right to Awareness & Consciousness;
Right to be Grateful

Northeast:
Right to Equitable Exchange; Right to Completion & Closure

West:
Right to Assess & Change

Center:
Right to Transform & Evolve; Right to Unconditional Love

East:
Right to Be

Southwest:
Right to Make Mistakes

Southeast:
Right to Learn

South:
Right to Grow;
Right to Work

Figure 4

The Rights of All Beings make up a holistic, interconnected system that describes the inborn, inalienable rights of all. These rights represent the lessons we humans must learn and practice in order to live in harmony with the rest of existence. They are the key to sustained survival. They are a source of profound joy, as well.

Today, we may face a great deal more complexity in our lives than these ancient people did. Yet, at the core, the issue is the same: How can we live in greater harmony with our world? In some very important ways, the conditions in which these ancients lived were not so different from our own. We are depleting all of our resources, and the lives of other species and many humans are considered expendable. Perhaps we can take heart from the idea that it was not a bolt of enlightenment that prompted early humans to consider how they might learn to live in such a way that life was sustainable; it was their near obliteration. We are in a similar place today.

The early indigenous people of whom we speak were more allegorical. They articulated their philosophical system through myth and story. What follows is a modern interpretation of these ancient truths. Let's now explore each of these rights and their meanings for us humans.

East: The Right to Be

The Universal Law of the Right to Be is the foundation for all the other rights. The law states that everything that exists has the right to exist. Every idea, person, invention, religion, plant, creature, inanimate object, environment, or country that exists has the right to be here. We may disagree with some of these, thinking them worthless or intolerable, but none of that matters. They have the inherent right to exist, given to them by the Universe. We need to abide by this, according all things this right. When we do so, energy flows freely. When we do not, energy is blocked, and there are consequences.

All other rights proceed from the Universal Law of the Right to Be.

Southeast: The Right to Learn

Each and every being has the right to learn whatever they need to learn during their existence in order to develop and realize their innate potential.

In exchange for this Right, the Universe asks us to discover whatever it is we don't know, but need to know. It asks us to commit to learning what we need to learn, and to practice receptivity to new learning. It asks us to listen to everyone and everything that has wisdom concerning the existing situation. Who is it that we can and should learn from? Who can help with this issue we are involved with?

South: The Right to Grow; The Right to Work

Growth is a requisite part of existence. If something cannot grow, it will stagnate and cease to exist. Therefore, everything that exists must have the Right to Grow.

In practice, the Rights to Learn and Grow mean we must allow all beings, including ourselves, to learn and grow in accordance with their unique process. These Rights ask us not to dominate or unnecessarily control the process, or judge the speed or method by which another learns. We humans need to nurture these learning and growing processes for others. In turn, we must be supported in our learning processes. If we do not receive appropriate support and nurturance in our learning process, our health, well-being, and very existence is imperiled.

The practice of these rights is fundamental to parental responsibility. As parents and teachers, we share responsibility in fostering our children, and those in our care. As mature adults, we are responsible for our self and, to a degree, others in context to agree-upon training.

The Rights to Learn and Grow are essential to any support system. In brief, they are the primary way by which we create the structure of a support system. This comes down to the Right to Work. Work is necessary for learning to be integrated, so growth can occur. All beings need to do this. For humans, this can look like practicing a musical instrument, or an analytical process. It can be the process of refining, or developing a particular tool, machine, or skill. It also opens the way for a being to be able to exchange and continue the energetic flow of their personal Circle, as well as participate in the Greater Circle.

Southwest: The Right to Make Mistakes

Just as Nature's "mistakes" are her way of "learning" what works and what doesn't, all beings have the right to make mistakes. No being should fear making a mistake.

One of our human factors is that we strive for perfection, even though the ideal is unattainable for humans. In practice, this Right asks us to accept our mistakes, and those of others, and not to expect idyllic perfection from others or ourselves. Mistakes are a wealth of information as to what doesn't work. Scientists and inventors are dependent on this hard-won knowledge. Thomas A. Edison is renowned for publicly acknowledging the importance of mistakes and failures.

West: The Right to Assess and Change

In the natural order, change is a constant. It is an essential aspect of survival. There is adaptation and mutation based on feedback from the environment, and experience.

This right says that all beings have the right to make periodic assessments and to make minor or significant changes based on those assessments. This right reminds us to embrace this process whenever it occurs in our own lives, and to honor this process in others as well. It's important to allow, expect, and encourage this aspect of the learning process. No one should feel that they do not have the freedom to change; nor should anyone be forced by another to remain the same.

This right also reminds us to anticipate change, and to value those things that help us change for the better. By this criterion, we are able to use our so-called "failures" (and those of others) as rich sources of feedback. We can also view our accomplishments with gratitude.

Northwest: The Right to Awareness & Consciousness; The Right to be Grateful

We have the right to develop increasingly higher levels of awareness and consciousness. This includes developing understandings that are not only intellectual, but also experiential. We have the right to aspire to understanding what works, and what doesn't, and why. We have the right to say that the "Emperor is wearing no clothes," even if everyone else says that he is. We have the right to gratefully acknowledge what is, and what is not, without fear of reprisal.

All beings have the right to experience the goodness in life, and to be grateful. The satisfaction and full belly a predator experiences after a successful hunt is a form of gratitude. Our process of spinning our straw into gold leaves us with much to be grateful for.

Our culture is very mental; it's based in mental energy. Sometimes we forget that we have the right to acquire and trust the sense of awareness that comes from and through our bodies. This is a legitimate source of knowledge, and we have the right to develop it. It can be the gateway to true wisdom, which is an even deeper level of integrated understanding.

North: The Right to Wisdom; The Right to Die

We all have the right to attain true wisdom. The Right to Wisdom is placed in the North, the place of age, and associated experience. In cultures facing constant survival challenges, wisdom was highly venerated. They realized that wisdom was a survival skill. Certain ritualistic experiences, such as vision quests, embody the respect that is accorded gaining wisdom.

With this right come responsibilities, those of guardianship and exemplarship. Those who attain wisdom ideally become guardians of the principles they know to be important and true. They must teach others how to live in accordance with these principles through some form of communication, whether it be written, verbal, signed or by example. They must pass it on.

The Right to Die says that every being has the right to go through the entire cycle of their beingness, which includes the resulting transformational process at the end of their existence. As humans, this Right teaches us that we must revere all stages of the process of life equally, including the final stage: death. Death is the ultimate transmutation, a process in which our physical vessel returns back to basic elements and becomes part of the earth, while our spirit returns into the non-physical realm from which we came. We tend to fear death, and thus we push it out of our consciousness. As a result, few of us prepare for death in a fully conscious way. This right teaches us to accept death as a natural part of the process, and to become more conscious of how we deal with it. The Right to Die includes the right to die with dignity, in a way of one's choosing. For example, you may put yourself in battle by choice. Elders had the right to go off and release themselves from their Earth Robes. This is a different way of looking at dying than that to which most of us are accustomed. They lived in serious situations that made death part of daily life. They experienced that the spirit did not die, but went on. They believed that death was a closure, and gave greater value to the journey of life. They were describing how they experienced the Greater Circle and flow that includes life and death.

Northeast: The Right to Equitable Exchange; The Right to Completion and Closure

The Right to Equitable Exchange states that all beings have the right to experience life as a continuous process of giving and receiving, in equal measure. This is the basis of the cycle of the universe. We have the accompanying responsibility to do our part to make sure that all the exchanges in which we're involved are mutually beneficial and equitable—not just beneficial for one party or interest. According to this right, all beings have the right to experience, and understand that they are valued. We each have the right to give and the right to receive, and should seek to balance the equation at every opportunity.

All beings need closure and completion; it is a right. Humans need ceremonies and rituals that mark and celebrate these completions. This includes at the end/death of a project, process, or even entity, such as a person or business. Human beings often fear death and closure, because it's the realm of the unknown as well as the space of no return. Completion rituals help us cope with that anxiety.

In this process we experience the satisfaction of completing something, of bringing something to fruition, and obtaining some acknowledgement of that. Our culture ignores this, much to our peril. Without proper closure, or being able to say good-bye, we are left hanging: the cycle of energy remains incomplete. With this type of energy leak, it is much harder to get ready for a new beginning.

Center: The Right to Transform and Evolve

This Right says that every being, whether sentient or not, has the right to go through the entire cycle of their existence. For non-sentient beings, this means from creation, to maturation, to dissolution of the physical structure, as we know it. For sentient beings, this means from birth, to the end of life, the dissolution of the physical structure, and the transition of the spirit. All of these processes help evolve consciousness for the benefit of the Whole, as well as for the individual.

The Right to Transform and Evolve is a process for all of life and existence. We go around the Circle many times in the course of a lifetime and, each time we will each experience endings and lesser "deaths." As humans, we will leave behind old ideas, beliefs, habits, relationships, and ways of making a living that no longer serve us. This is natural and appropriate. We must respect these passages both in ourselves and in others. We must accept that sometimes we—or others—must let go and move on as our personal evolution demands. So it is that parents must accept that their children must create lives of their own. Beliefs that have been the underpinnings of our entire lives may need to be transformed. Relationships in which we have become heavily invested must sometimes end for the greater good of all concerned.

Evolution is the natural order of the Universe. It is occurring all the time, as an integral part of the ongoing flow. And what is the goal of evolution? We want there to be a perfect, final goal. The primitives believed greater "consciousness" to be the goal, however nebulous that may seem. All of creation goes through a multitude of beginnings and endings, constantly seeking greater clarity and understanding.

The process of evolution is often challenging to us humans. We want to hold onto things as they are, hide out, or escape from the inescapable. But, as always, difficult things go easier when we move toward them, accept them, and learn to flow with them. By attending to each of these inevitable evolutionary challenges as they arise, success is assured.

The "Engine": The Right to Unconditional Love

All beings have the Right to Unconditional Love. We have the right to participate in the Universal Flow of Energy, and to receive nurturance from this type of support. Nurturance is the Universe's expression of unconditional love. All beings need and deserve nurturance. It's what helps keep the Universal Flow going. There are no set conditions, inclusive of our engaging with the opportunity, or not. It is the individual's responsibility to take in the nurturance available.

Human beings also have the innate ability to practice unconditional love. We often get invested in illusions and distractions that tell us a false story about what love is, and what it's supposed to look like. Our experience of love is generally *conditional*. We have a tendency to put attachments, investments, and/or conditions on our love. When we do this, we make it hard for others to engage with our love. The result is that we don't get back the love we want and deserve. We can break out of this destructive cycle.

~ Business Revolution through Ancestral Wisdom ~

If we want to truly engage with Universal Flow, our easiest door is Unconditional Love. By practicing Unconditional Love through nurturing and supporting the Right to Be of others and ourselves, we receive the support and nurturance of Universal Flow. When we don't practice this, we cut ourselves off from the source of energy. This is why Unconditional Love is the "engine"—because it's what keeps the Circle moving.

We manifest unconditional love when we practice:

- True acceptance of all
- Equitability in our dealings with others
- *Being willing to compromise,* rather than insisting on our way
- Allowing others their developmental journeys
- Being accountable for our actions which, in turn, affect other beings and the Earth

The Rights of All Beings are universal. They are encoded in the nature of the universe. They are innate to all things that exist. Tu and Láné's contribution is to articulate these Rights, showing how they work with the directions on the Circle. "The awareness of this universal code comes from observing the natural world," says Láné. "When you really look and see how everything works cooperatively, you learn how balance is maintained through the relationship of all things to each other: a tree relating to a rock, relating to the soil, relating to a bird, relating to the sky, and all relating to each other. Our ancestors saw this. From observation we can see they're all letting each other be, as well as being nurtured and supported in the process. When we get further and further away from the natural order and way of being, we lose that perspective."

These Rights of Beingness provide us with a very high set of personal standards for how we conduct ourselves as human beings. These standards are not to be set aside when we enter the world of business.

~ Business Revolution through Ancestral Wisdom ~

The Rights of All Beings in Business

Note that there are some differences in this Circle, due to the specific needs of business, as we will explain.

The Rights of All Beings as Applied to Business

North:
Right to Wisdom;
Right to Closure & Completion

Northwest:
Right to Full Awareness;
Right to Share Gratitude

Northeast:
Right to Equitable Exchange

West:
Right to Assess & Change

Center:
Right to Evolve;
Right to Engage with Transition & Transformation

East:
Right to Be

Southwest:
Right to Make Mistakes

Southeast:
Right to Learn

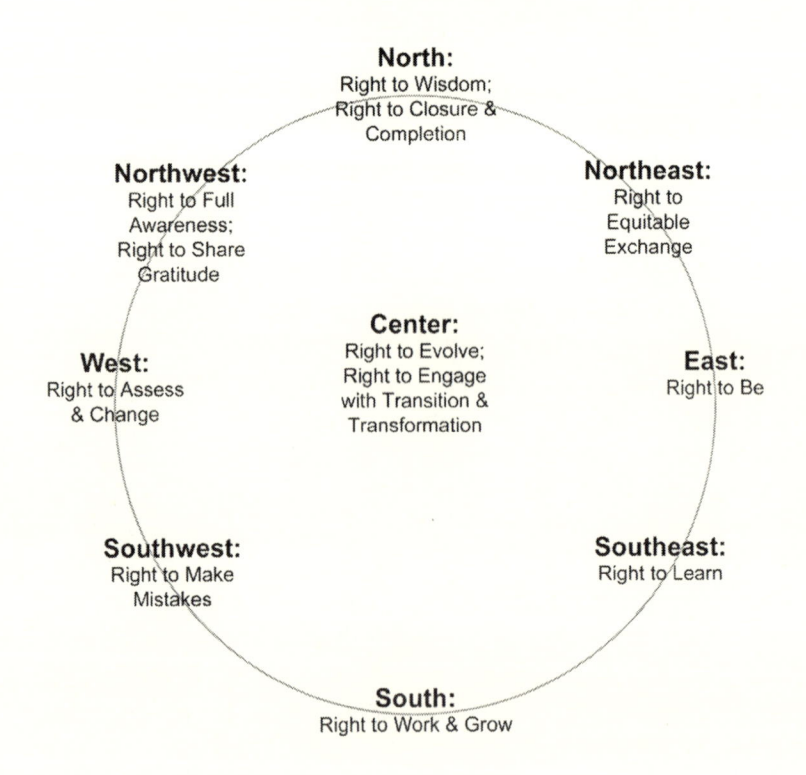

South:
Right to Work & Grow

Figure 5

East: The Right to Be

- Just as every human has the Right to Be, every human also has the right to create a business. This is their right, whether they be female, poor, a minority, or all three. We do not have the right to deprive anyone of his/her right to prosperity or livelihood.

- Every business has the right to be: It has the right to be created and to exist, ongoingly. Therefore, our competition also has the right to exist. We must not interfere with that right.

- Everyone involved in your business has the right to exist. They should consciously give that right to the business and to themselves, as well.

- Your customers have the Right to Be, and so do their needs and wants.

We live in accordance with the Right to Be by consciously acknowledging and accepting the right to be of all these beings, even when—especially when--it's challenging or difficult for us. This always frees more energy, and contributes to the cycle of life.

Southeast: The Right to Learn

The Right to Learn begins in the Southeast where you do the preparatory work to bring the concept into reality. We have the right and responsibility to learn whatever is required to make our business a success. Sometimes there can be barriers to bringing about our vision. We must persevere through them, while still allowing the blockages the right to exist, and learning how to get through them. We just don't have to engage with them, or focus on them to our detriment.

South: The Right to Work & Grow

- Every business has the right to open its doors.

- Every business resource, and very person involved with the business, has the right to develop and grow.

- Everyone has the right to work.

The South is where we set to work to prove our concept. At this point, we are fully committed, but we must also stay mindful and practice moderation. Many of our bad habits start to surface here, as we start to realize results. The reality test begins here.

Southwest: The Right to Make Mistakes

We have a right to make mistakes. It's part of learning and growing, as a valuable part of the process. This means in the Southwest we get serious about adopting a proper attitude about mistakes. We release any investment we have in being right. We resolve not to over-dramatize, or beat ourselves up because we made a mistake; we resolve not to bring the business down because mistakes were made. Then we put a process in place that ensures that we:

- Identify any mistakes that occur in a timely manner.

- Acknowledge mistakes openly to whoever has the right to know. (Don't cover up or hide the mistake, and don't pretend everything is "OK.")

- Evaluate the impact of those mistakes.

- Make amends for the mistake to anyone who was injured by it.

- Create a safe way for people to make suggestions for improvement.

West: The Right to Assess & Change

- Make adjustments and changes to help your business continuously improve.

- Create a process that best enables continuous improvement.

- Plan to conduct periodic overall evaluations of the business with an eye to learning what needs to change in the business in order to achieve better results.

- Identify any important misassumptions and/or mistakes.

- Share your findings openly, with both employees and shareholders.

- Institute the suggestion process to make it a vital part of the assessment process.

The process of assessment and change are ongoing in a business. They are important for keeping up with the demands and competition. Make this a straightforward process, with no blame or recriminations. Focus on what worked, and what didn't work. By acknowledging jobs well done publicly, you can make this a positive and rewarding process.

Northwest: The Right to Full Awareness; The Right to Share Gratitude

Every person in a business has the right to full awareness about the status of the business, and the information that affects their performance. As a business leader your responsibility is to share that information. Make sure that you have a good line of communication between you, your employees, the community, and any others involved.

We have a tendency to hold back on providing feedback until a performance review. Obviously, this is not optimal, as timely constructive communication helps workers develop their experience base, and this benefits the business. The Right to Full Awareness helps us remember that workers have a right to ongoing feedback. In addition, the feedback should not just focus on what isn't working well (*i.e.,* we should not just focus on giving negative feedback). In the spirit of full awareness, we should also provide positive feedback about what *is* working. When feedback is continuous, it gives us more opportunities to pass on the wisdom of "best practices." This keeps everyone continuously learning, and the business constantly improving.

Although the experience of gratitude begins in the West, it is here in the transition to the North that we fully engage with it. Humans, and businesses alike, need positive acknowledgement.

North: The Right to Wisdom; The Right to Completion & Closure

Note that, in the context of business, the Right to Completion & Closure is in the North, the place of wisdom. This is because this Right is for a business what the Right to Die is for humans and other sentient beings: These are significant passages that inform, and are informed by, wisdom. This is why the process of closure and completion should begin in the North, though it won't be finalized until we reach the East direction.

Most businesses experience multiple completions and closures over their lifespan. Many of these occur on the basis of the calendar, with completions occurring at regular intervals. The business, and everyone associated with it, has the right to experience these necessary completions and closures in a timely fashion, so they can move on with renewed energy. You express these Rights in your Business when you:

- Share what you are learning with your subsidiaries and your alliances by passing on wisdom, inclusive of "best practices." In so doing you start building the exemplarship capacity of your process as a business.

- Share in some appropriate way with the environment. This demonstrates your ongoing commitment to the local community, as well as the natural resources we are all dependent upon.

- Consider how you might exhibit exemplarship in the community.

- Remember to prepare for the next cycle by bringing conscious awareness to the completion of projects and processes. Give acknowledgement where acknowledgement is due, to build strength and loyalty within your business and community.

- Set up the conditions that allow people to come to closure. If it's necessary to stop or close something prematurely, alert employees early so that the closure of the plant or business doesn't shock them. For example, if a certain store in your chain isn't making enough money, alert employees in the Southwest, when you first discover the problem. Enlist their participation by asking for input and ideas. Can we turn it around? This kind of management creates tremendous loyalty. This kind of management engenders mutual respect and appreciation.

Everyone has the right to pursue and acquire wisdom. Those who acquire it through experience deserve great respect. Their voice must be sought and heeded. In turn, those who acquire wisdom need to practice the discipline of integrity, as they are living examples for others. They become the guardians of the principles and values of the group. By teaching others through example, one begins the process of passing on one's wisdom. By passing the wisdom on to the next person, we bring completion and closure to our work, and to our lives. We ensure sustainability.

Northeast: The Right to Equitable Exchange–

Everyone and everything involved with your business has the right to equitable exchange. This means that mutually beneficial equitable exchange should be the goal of *all* business transactions. It means we need to be accountable for our actions: We need to look at both the short- and long-term effect on other beings and the earth. Businesses must ask:

- What is the business's responsibility to its people and community?

- What is the business's responsibility in terms of an equitable exchange with the earth for resources used or consumed?

A business can physically demonstrate mutually beneficial exchanges by:

- Having appropriate salaries. The relationship between CEO salaries and the wages of workers need to be more balanced. CEO's should expect to put in more hours and be more responsible. They should not have runaway salaries. Workers need to be able to make a living, without needing another job.

- Salary raises—no matter how small--should be shared at all levels of the business. This includes the CEO as well as all workers, if they have earned it.

- You begin to repay everyone that helped you get started, including all your alliances and supporters/suppliers, and the community in which you are embedded.

- You begin to work with the community in more depth by sharing wealth and/or gifts of wisdom through workshops, a bequeathing process, etc.

In addition, you honor the Right of Completion and Closure in the North, and prepare for a new cycle beginning in the East by:

- Building in activities such as end-of-year parties, gifts, and bonuses. Sponsor celebrations when projects are completed. People need a sense of fulfillment and satisfaction.

Center: The Right to Evolve and Become (*i.e.*, The Right to Engage with Transition and Transformation)

Just as every human has the right to evolve and become, so does every business. As a business leader you need to consciously shepherd that process. That means you need to be consciously aware of the stage of evolution your business is currently in as well as the stage it will enter into next *before* it enters that stage. You need to be prepared for your business to fundamentally change. You need to regularly ask questions such as:

- What is in the best interests of all involved, including the natural environment?

- How do we see the business evolving?

- What could it become, if it became all it could be?

- What effect would that have on the world and future generations?

Center: The Right to Unconditional Love

Businesses honor the right of all beings to unconditional nurturance, support, and acceptance when we:

- Look for exchanges (*i.e.,* business transactions) that benefit all parties equitably.

- Are *willing to compromise,* rather than insisting on our way.

- Support the aspirations and development of our employees.

- Interact with each other in a respectful way, regardless of our stage in life.

- Take accountability for our actions because we acknowledge that our actions have an effect on other beings and the Earth. As the wisdom of the Iroquois nation teaches us: What will be the effect seven generations forward?

These rights and responsibilities provide us with a set of standards for how to conduct business. High standards encourage us to reach toward how we want to be; they connect us with something infinite, something much larger than ourselves. Our business is provided with a strong, adaptable structure of integrity.

Business is a part of life—not a separate realm with its own rules. The Rights of All Beings tell us what will really work to ensure our own survival, as well as that of our businesses. They are a gift from the indigenous people of the world. They are a gift from our ancestors.

Chapter Seven
The Circle Process in Business

The Circle and its nine directions provide a powerful process that human beings can use in their creation of anything. The Circle sets people on a course of action that naturally replicates the spiral of evolution. Each turn around the Circle represents a new stage in the evolution of the process.

~ Business Revolution through Ancestral Wisdom ~

The Universal Blueprint

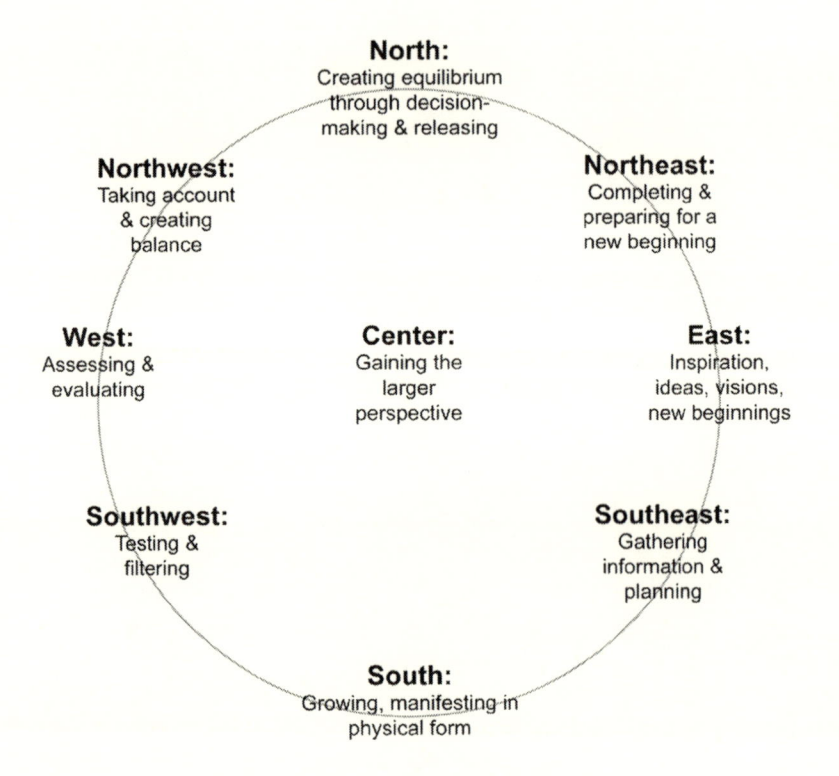

North: Creating equilibrium through decision-making & releasing

Northwest: Taking account & creating balance

Northeast: Completing & preparing for a new beginning

West: Assessing & evaluating

Center: Gaining the larger perspective

East: Inspiration, ideas, visions, new beginnings

Southwest: Testing & filtering

Southeast: Gathering information & planning

South: Growing, manifesting in physical form

Figure 6

The Nine Directions and their Meanings for Business

• The Energy of the East (or place of individuation) –

We begin in the East.[16] The East is where the sun rises. This visual sighting is the start of our connection with the sun. Everything that exists in the physical realm begins with a vision, an illumination, an idea, or an inspiration that comes into our minds from the Source (*i.e.,* the unknown influence, or flow of

~ 152 ~

energy from other than ourselves). The East direction represents that energy, where those ideas begin to take shape and form.

This direction speaks about the first moments of illumination, the dawning of a new idea, the moment when we awaken and remember a dream that shapes our future. The East direction reminds us how important it is to periodically open ourselves up to all the information that is available to guide us in our lives. We often shut down out of self-protection; the Eastern direction reminds us that that there are points in our lives when it's important—even necessary—to be open, to trust that the wisdom we need is always available to us if we are open to it. It encourages us to honor even seemingly insignificant feelings, ideas, or images. These can turn out to be important carriers of wisdom. The Eastern direction also reminds us to exercise moderation, as we can be overwhelmed by the multitude of possibilities and opportunities that present themselves to us.

As the East is where the sun starts its ascent upward from the horizon, we intuitively associate it with new beginnings, and the place where things start. This direction is where we lay the foundation for everything that comes after, making it an important type of creative energy.

In business, each activity starts in the East direction. We engage with this energy as a source of inspiration, calling forth new ideas and visions, and setting the stage for new beginnings. It is here we create structural outlines and define goals. It is here that we lay the foundation that sets the manifestation process in motion. Typical questions we address in the East direction include:

- What is my vision for my business?
- What new ideas or concepts am I inspired to develop?

• The Energy of the Southeast –

The Southeast represents the energy required to bring any inspiration, vision, or new idea into physical reality. It's a transitional energy. It's associated with the gathering of resources, both intellectual and material, that are needed in order to manifest a vision in the world. It reminds us that we must do a significant amount of research and planning; before something can be built, many things have to be thoroughly investigated and thought through. This is also where you need to do an honest assessment of your business's potential, as well as your ability to accomplish what's needed. You must determine whether you have access to sufficient resources, and whether you, personally, are willing and able to put forth the personal effort required.

This is a very crucial point in the process. How well you respond will determine whether the energy stops or surges forward into the project. You need to be diligent and disciplined.

The tasks and questions you'll need to address in the Southeast include the following:

- Assessing the potential of your business idea: What is the market potential? What is the competition, and how does my idea stack up?
- Researching and Planning: What are the requirements for success? What information is needed? What tasks are required? What questions must be thought through?
- Taking Stock of your Resource Requirements: What will it take to actually implement this idea? What do you need in terms of equipment, finances, personnel, and other resources? What required resources do you have? Do you have all your backers and any other necessary allies in place?
- Performing a Feasibility Assessment: Can you realistically acquire those things you need? What is the likelihood of success?
- Mustering the Needed Resources: Can you actually obtain the support you need, including the important alliances, backers, capital funds, suppliers, and supplies? What other resources might we need?
- Conducting a Personal Assessment/Reality Check: What's required from you personally to both create and run this

business? Do you, personally, have what it takes to carry out this vision?

The work you do in the Southeast is akin to a readiness assessment. If you decide you're ready, then you're set to move to the South, where you put your plan into action.

• **The Energy of the South –**

As the earth moves around the sun, morning gives way to the full light of day. The South direction represents midday and summer, the time when things come into full bloom. It also represents the time of young adulthood, when we are most active, building our careers and families. The South represents the energy that we perceive when we observe a growing garden, a honeycomb, an anthill, or a factory at full tilt. It's the place of action, of building, growing, and manifesting in physical reality.

In a business, you are engaged with South direction energy when you are:

- Obtaining funding
- Hiring people
- Setting up the business, and opening your doors
- Creating or delivering your product, or performing your service

This is the part of the business that many of us love the most. In fact, our culture has such an affinity for this energy that we tend to lose sight of the process as a whole. We often think the process of creation is complete at this stage.

Typical questions addressed in the South include:

- Are all the business functions and supports in place for me to open shop? Do we have adequate funding? Do we have

the equipment and suppliers we need? Do we have sufficient workforce?
- Are we meeting market demand? Are we completing orders on time?
- Have we marketed effectively?
- What is the competition doing?

• The Energy of the Southwest—

The Southwest represents another transition place. The first objective is to discover any snafus. This is where you take your idea, your option, your vision, process, or product and you mature it. You push it to where you want to go in order to test it, to see if there are any problems. This is your proving ground. You prove to yourself and others that you are ready to consistently turn out quality goods or services—or not. If you find problems, then you take steps to filter them out. That's the second objective: to refine your products or processes. Here, you tinker, trying out new options, and making adjustments until you are satisfied, and ready to go forward.

In business terms, the Southwest direction is where you:

- Do your first quality checking; work on consistency in your product or service
- Market and sell your product; set conditions for the release of work completed; present your finished work and application of work
- Detect any problems or snafus
- Try out new remedies; test new options

Note that the Southwest direction is where problems and obstacles first surface. Discovering a problem is sometimes a bit difficult emotionally. Because the Circle builds this discovery step into the process, you are much less likely to experience discouragement. The Circle process helps you anticipate and plan for these necessary adjustments. Questions associated with this direction include:

- Is my product or service living up to the standards of quality in the marketplace? How consistently are we meeting these quality standards? Are there variations that need to be addressed?
- How effective is our quality control? What improvements are needed or wanted?
- What snafus have occurred? Where have they occurred? How should we address them, so that they don't occur in the future?

• The Energy of the West –

The sun sets in the West, and inspires us to step back, reflect, and review the day. The energy of the West is autumnal energy: a place of introspection, assessment, and evaluation what has occurred before. The West is also the place of maturation and harvest, where we reap what we have sown, both the good and the bad.

In business terms, the Western direction energy asks us to assess and evaluate. It's about taking the time to conduct necessary, major reviews of your progress thus far toward your original vision. You also look at the results of your quality testing in the Southwest, and ask: Are there larger implications? For example, the testing phase in the Southwest can surface areas of conflict. In the West, you would consider how you might re-prioritize, or choose between options to resolve those conflicts. Based on the feedback received, it is here that we start to develop new instructions or plans. The West also reminds us to conduct major maintenance on our buildings and/or machines.

The West reminds us to ask questions like the following:

- Of the new options we've tested (in the Southwest), which look the most promising?
- How is our business really doing? How is it doing

externally? What does our customer feedback say about our performance? How is it doing internally? Is there high employee morale and work satisfaction?
- Do certain aspects of our business (e.g., customer service, assembly line, collections, quality assurance, etc.) seem to need improvements or adjustments?
- What was the impact of certain policies and/or decisions on various aspects of the business, e.g., marketing, sales, factory workers, suppliers, profits?
- What has been the effect of our recent change initiative? What has occurred as a result?

• The Energy of the Northwest—

The Northwest is another transitional energy. As the seasons shift from autumn to winter, all the living beings take stock of their stores, and prepare for the future. This is where we do a true accounting, which tells us whether we're operating on an even keel or not. Part of that process is our acknowledgement of both our successes and our mistakes.

Our overall objective is to create greater *balance*. We want to look at the balance sheet with an eye toward creating greater internal consistency and harmony. This means we want to note any extremes that occurred, and recommend a more balanced course of action for the future. Opting for balance doesn't mean we always choose the middle road or lack spice in our lives. It just means that, overall, we strive to live a balanced and harmonious life.

Translated into the business world, the Northwest energy reminds you to accumulate all the necessary information so you may take stock of both your business and yourself. Now, you can refine and plan for what changes, if any, need to be made.

In the East you began with a vision. Now, you're more than halfway around the Circle; your vision has been implemented in the "real world." Your goal at this juncture is to determine what you need to do to arrive at a rewarding balance between your original vision and ideals, and any practical concerns that have arisen. After your assessment and evaluation in the West, you'll have some sense of where your business stands with regard to profitability and other external measures. The next step is to gather feedback. The information you gather will help you do a true, honest, and comprehensive accounting.

To develop an even fuller picture of your business, you'll want to reach out and seek input about potential improvements and refinements. You want this from the people involved with and/or impacted by the business (employees, suppliers, clients, partners, people in the community, etc.). You'll want to listen to your employees' suggestions and ideas regarding your products, processes, or service delivery methods. The output is a set of recommendations designed to help create greater balance. Along the way, you'll also want to acknowledge and reward the people who have done a great job over the past year. This practice helps create balance on the energetic plane, as well.

In sum, the Northwest is a place of inclusion and integration for greater internal coherence. Questions associated with the Northwest include:

- What kind of information do we need to inform our decisions? Who do we need to survey?
- What suggestions or ideas do our employees have?
- How can we find a balance between our original vision and practical concerns? What does resolution look like? What specific recommendations need to be formulated? Is an attitude adjustment of some kind in order?

• **The Energy of the North –**

The North direction is the place of midnight and winter. It is when the fields go fallow. Not much happens on the surface, but underground, the sources of new life gather. The energy of the North is about discernment, and moving into a more quiescent, inner-focused stage. In this way, the North direction represents a place of resolution. We decide whether to commit to something, or release it. This process of sorting, committing, and releasing returns us to equilibrium. The energy of the North can guide us when we need to settle issues, make decisions, close chapters, and release that which is no longer useful or needed. We always carry with us the knowledge that endings contain the seeds of new beginnings. Life goes on, and the cycle continues—but first you have to let go. This is what we learn from the North.

In the North direction resolution is the goal, and decision-making is the core process. In the Northwest, your goal was to accumulate all the information you needed to make informed decisions. Now, you make those decisions, based on the outcome of your evaluation process. You may choose to express your resolve through commitments. You may decide to affirm previous goals and ideals, and/or make a new set that will carry over into a new cycle. You may need to let go of some things you once thought were vital, that no longer serve the business. This is not always easy as we become invested in our ideas, but doing so frees blocked energy. The North, then, is also a place of power: there is great power in making commitments, and coming to a place of resolution.

Since the Northern direction stands for a time of natural dormancy, you may find yourself in a similar energetic field when facing difficult decisions. You may need to make some significant changes. These may include changing some of the fundamental assumptions the business is based upon. You may need to restructure, contract, or even close your business. These prospects can be very unsettling, and you may be tempted to go to sleep (metaphorically speaking) or disappear in some way, rather than face the decision squarely. Obviously, this is not in your best interest as you will not create the resolution your business and its people need.

The Circle helps by providing us with a process that enables us to anticipate these difficult moments. Therefore, we are more prepared for them. Remember that the North is the place of wisdom, and can be a tremendous ally. It can guide us in our process of resolution, decision-making, commitment, and closure.

The North is where we seek help in letting go of those things that no longer serve us, *i.e.,* the extremes, the imbalances, and the inequities. It can lead us to greater clarity, understanding, and expertise.

Questions to ask in the North direction include:

- Now that we have evaluated the state of the business, what decisions need to be made?
- Based on our evaluation and the feedback of our employees, will we make recommended changes to our policies and procedures?
- After reviewing the results of this initiative, do we continue our commitment to it?
- Are we taking adequate care of our employees? Are they enrolled in retirement and health plans, etc.?
- What else may be required to create resolution or equilibrium?

• The Energy of the Northeast—

The Northeast is the fourth transitional energy; it holds the space of passage to a new cycle. Here you prepare to begin again at a different (higher) level, by bringing closure to the old cycle. The energy is contemplative: we look back to see if we've missed anything that needs to be addressed before closing the old cycle.

Completion is important. One of the best ways to create closure is by sharing what we have gained over the past cycle. We share our prosperity with the community of those who have supported us in achieving this abundance. Our prosperity is directly proportionate to the level of help we have achieved from our community of supporters: family, friends, employees, resources, and the Earth. This sharing may take many forms. We might dispense money, material goods, personal wisdom, or even useful new business ideas that we offer to the surrounding community through workshops. We might restore a local stream, or greenbelt.

The sharing of prosperity facilitates our letting go of the past, in order to make room for the new. It also signifies that we acknowledge that there is a larger process unfolding—the universal process of manifestation. Sharing signifies that we are participating consciously in that process, and that we are grateful for the support we have received thus far.

In the Northeast you ask yourself questions such as:

- What is needed to prepare the ground, before we set out on this new course of action? What have we forgotten to attend to?
- How might we share/give back from our bounty to the Earth, and the community that supports our business?

• Returning to the East--

We must always close our Circle by returning to the East where we begin a new cycle from a place of more experience.

Before we start a new cycle, we may decide that it's appropriate to engage with the energy at the Center of the Circle. If so, we still must return to the East energy first, even just momentarily. It enables us to collect ourselves from the cyclical journey we have just finished before engaging with the powerful energy of the Center. This is appropriate and necessary.

• The Energy of the Center—

The Center of the Circle represents another very distinct kind of energy. It's the place of evolution and of leadership. It reminds us to seek a larger perspective, to look at the big picture, and to get a sense of the overall effectiveness of our efforts. Here, before commencing a new cycle, we pause to re-connect with our vision and consider the likely ramifications of our actions and choices over the long-term. We consider how the business wants to grow and evolve: we focus on the role that leadership needs to play in bringing that potential to fruition.

We turn to the energy of the Center when, as leaders, we need to re-charge our vision or redesign major aspects of our business. Because the Center facilitates this larger view, it's an especially powerful energy.

In business, the questions to ask when we are in the Center include the following:

- Are we achieving our vision?
- Are the goals we set still worthwhile?
- What are the possible effects and repercussions of these new actions we're about to take?
- What is the next step in the evolution of this company?
- What kind of leadership are we promoting through our words and actions? How effective is our leadership? How does our leadership need to evolve?
- Are we approaching things in an altruistic way?

• Beginning Again in the East--

Once we have taken the time and space to assess the entirety of the situation, it's time to begin again, resolving to put into place all that has been learned during our completed cycle. As we return to the East, we do not return to exactly the same place. If we have grown and evolved as a result of our conscious, circular process we begin again at a higher level. If we failed in our effort to proceed consciously, we may begin at a lower place because we have descended from where we were.

In either case, our circle path now begins to evolve into a spiral. Our movement, which we once thought was linear, now takes on a dynamically different form. Instead of feeling perpetually lost, in search of something unnamed and unknown, we have our bearings. We walk in relationship to ourselves, past and future, and we walk in relationship to all there is in the universe.

The Wisdom of the Circle Process

Through the nine different directions, the Circle enables us to work with nine different facets of our reality. The energetic requirements of each of the steps are unique, requiring their own particular skills, tasks, and mindsets. As we work our way around the Circle, we experience each of these perspectives. We experience all nine facets, and we see how they inter-connect and inter-relate. This gives us a way to deal with both the parts and the whole at the same time. It is a balanced approach. The process is inherently holistic; and yet it's not overwhelmingly complex.

One turn around the Circle creates movement, moving as a spiral to generate creative energy. Because the Circle is a part of us, the process feels "natural." We easily orient to where we are in the process. Unlike linear processes, we can see our present state in relationship to previous and future cycles. As a result, we become grounded and present.

Each of the directions builds upon the one before. In this way, the Circle actually exemplifies cooperation. Each perspective *cooperates* with the next to provide us with a greater, and more in-depth perception of the whole. In life, we all have different predilections, preferences, and strengths. The Circle reminds us of the value of collaboration. It models the pooling of resources, the inclusion of others who have different skills or perspectives (some of which may be challenging to us, but are nonetheless necessary to comprehending the whole). This in and of itself makes the Circle valuable to humans.

Did you note the difference between the lower and upper halves of the Circle? The lower half of the Circle speaks to activities in the physical realm, whereas the upper half of the Circle represents activities in the non-physical realm. The lower half is the realm of action and physical manifestation. The upper half is the place of philosophy, the dreaming place, the place for planning for the future, for sharing with others, for reflecting and contemplating where to go next. Both are essential to wholeness, just as both halves are essential to the Circle process.

You might consider whether you, personally, have a tendency

to be more comfortable in one realm or the other. In general, the business world focuses on the physical realm. There is also an inherent bias toward action, and a tendency to be somewhat dismissive of reflection. Whenever we're out of balance we run the risk of getting into trouble. The Circle process ensures that we pay attention to both physical and non-physical realms.

Likewise, the right and left sides differ. The right side speaks to inspiration, vision, and planning. It's about creativity, dreams, and the generation of ideas. The left side speaks to the need to refine, evaluate, and change based on what we're learning about how our ideas are working (or not working) in reality. One might also say that the right side is more yang. The right side is active. It's about opening to inspiration (in-spirit). It brings these ideas into the mental (air) realm, and helps develop them into physical manifestation (earth). The left side is more yin, *i.e.,* reflective and evaluative. The left side helps us draw upon the grounded energy of the earth. It moves us into the realm of feeling in the West, and puts us in touch with the wisdom of the spiritual dimension in the North. It helps us to evaluate and make informed decisions. Both sides are equally important and necessary.

Many of us, however, have a tendency to favor one side over the other. If we favor the right half of the cycle, we focus on churning out new ideas and theories. If we don't honor the left side, we can be visionaries with little concern for the effects of our ideas. We shift the burden of implementing and testing our ideas onto others, rather than assuming the responsibility to evaluate and refine the ideas ourselves. If, on the other hand, we favor the left-hand side of the Circle we might tend to be critical. We may focus on what's lacking in any new idea, while not necessarily involving ourselves in the integrative process. We may even resent the idea-generators who appear to be jumping from new idea to new idea, leaving all the testing and refining to us.

Clearly, both of these semi-circle strategies are less than optimal. Both leave us with a fragmented result. Both rob us of that essential sense of wholeness. When we use the whole Circle process, however, our approach will be much more thorough and complete. The Circle marries vision with evaluation, and it unites the material realm with the province of spirit.[17] The Circle reminds us to include all aspects of the whole in our consideration, and it provides us with a process for doing so.

Several examples of how to use the Circle process are included in the **Appendix**. Many more will be included in Volume 2.

Chapter Eight
The Circle Process in Business

As a blueprint, the Circle is both complete and comprehensive. It's able to address all the different aspects of building, running, and evolving a business. The Circle can:

- Help us address all business-related tasks, issues, and concerns, because the Circle encompasses them all. Each of the nine directions represents a specific kind of energy, all of which are necessary to the conduct of business. The Circle hosts this robust toolbox of energies and gives us access to it.

- Put all of these tasks into a meaningful context that's comprehensive, but not overwhelming. This will help us stay organized and oriented.

- Help us stay aware of where we are in the overall process of building, running, or evolving a business. It grounds us in the moment, while reminding us to look at the long view and the big picture.

~ Business Revolution through Ancestral Wisdom ~

The Circle below provides an overview of what we mean.

The Circle as Applied to Business: The Beginning Steps

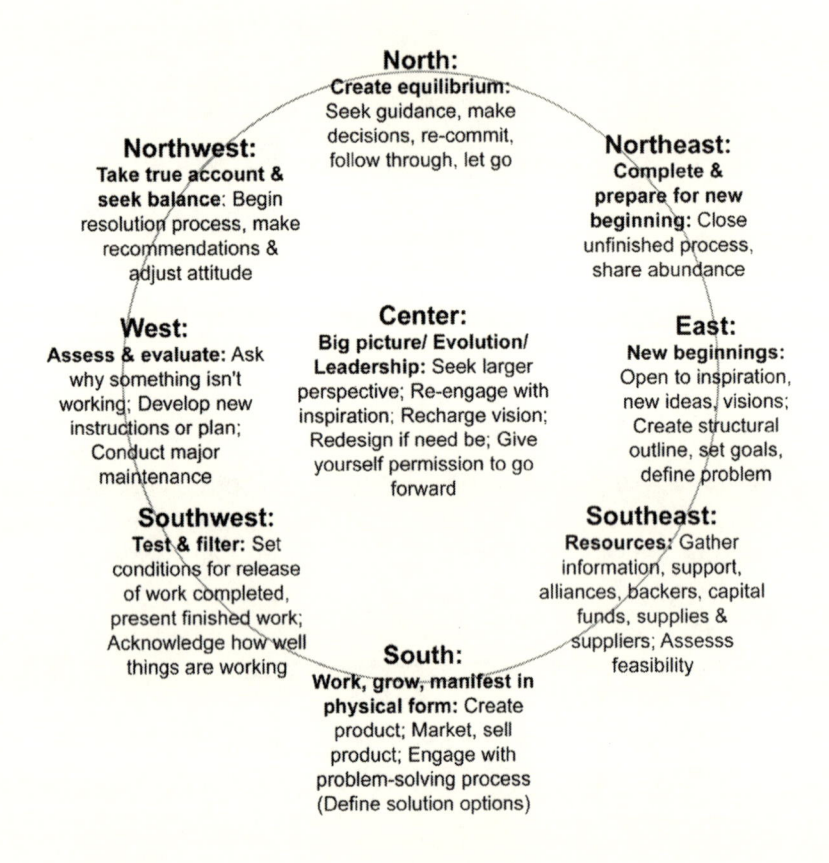

North:
Create equilibrium: Seek guidance, make decisions, re-commit, follow through, let go

Northwest:
Take true account & seek balance: Begin resolution process, make recommendations & adjust attitude

Northeast:
Complete & prepare for new beginning: Close unfinished process, share abundance

West:
Assess & evaluate: Ask why something isn't working; Develop new instructions or plan; Conduct major maintenance

Center:
Big picture/ Evolution/ Leadership: Seek larger perspective; Re-engage with inspiration; Recharge vision; Redesign if need be; Give yourself permission to go forward

East:
New beginnings: Open to inspiration, new ideas, visions; Create structural outline, set goals, define problem

Southwest:
Test & filter: Set conditions for release of work completed, present finished work; Acknowledge how well things are working

Southeast:
Resources: Gather information, support, alliances, backers, capital funds, supplies & suppliers; Assesss feasibility

South:
Work, grow, manifest in physical form: Create product; Market, sell product; Engage with problem-solving process (Define solution options)

Figure 7

How the Circle Helps Us Avoid Business Failure

A number of academic experts and business consultants have published their "top ten" or "top fifteen" causes of business failure. The Circle can help prevent these problems from arising by focusing our attention appropriately as we move through each direction. This results in a comprehensive approach. On the next few pages we show why this is so.

The **East** direction focuses us on:
- Developing a comprehensive vision for the business
- Establishing an ethical foundation (Universal Laws and Principles, And Rights)
- Aligning with Universal Energy, which is infinitely creative, from the beginning; managing creative energy effectively

This focus helps us avoid these common business problems:
- Lack of vision; inadequate vision
- No shared ethical base
- No fostering of creativity; insufficient innovation

The **Southeast** direction focuses us on:
- Researching and planning
- Acquiring necessary resources

This focus helps us avoid these common business problems:
- Poor planning (strategic and financial)
- Inadequate definition of customer base
- Inadequate understanding of competition
- Inadequate personnel/staffing
- Insufficient working capital

The **South** direction focuses us on:
- Managing the various aspects of the business, such as personnel, finances, marketing and the delivery of products and services so as to ensure productivity over the long-term

This focus helps us avoid these common business problems:
- Failure to adequately market product
- Employee/management turnover;
- Disruptions in key relationships (*i.e.,* with suppliers)
- Inventory issues

The **Southwest** direction puts our focus on:
- Testing and refining our ideas, products, and people;

~ Business Revolution through Ancestral Wisdom ~

aiming for consistent quality
- Identifying problems and mistakes early; the ability to learn from mistakes, and improve

This focus helps us avoid these common business problems:
- Inadequate quality; problems with quality control
- Inadequate control systems in general
- Inability to identify and deal with mistakes, failures, and/or problems without blaming and looking for scapegoats
- Inadequate customer service: not dealing well with customer dissatisfaction
- Cost over-runs; not controlling costs

The **West** direction puts our focus on:
- Implementing systems and processes for overall assessment and evaluation
- Resolving conflicts and problems as they occur

This focus helps us avoid these common business problems:
- Inadequate definition of success
- Measuring the wrong things or nothing; "flying blind"
- Inadequate accounting records

The **Northwest** direction puts our focus on:
- Gathering data and feedback from employees in preparation for decision-making
- Taking in information from both inside and outside the business
- Creating consistency and balance

This focus helps us avoid these common business problems:
- Insufficient data to support decisions
- Inadequate customer follow-up
- No team input in decision-making
- Not seeking information from outside re: competitive environment, change in customer preferences, etc.
- Inconsistencies within business
- Dissension within management ranks and between levels
- Burn-out: Long hours, stress, no fun

The **North** direction puts our focus on:
- Decision-making
- Flexibility; the ability to adapt and change
- Seeking guidance

This focus helps us avoid these common business problems:
- Poor decision-making practices (procrastination, trouble letting go, etc.)
- Lack of flexibility and versatility; inability to change in response to information
- Not seeking external professional help when necessary

The **Northeast** direction puts our focus on:
- Seeking feedback from the community, and processing to create closure, without judgment
- Sharing of abundance; replenishment of resources

This focus helps us avoid these common business problems:
- Disconnection from community; resentment by community
- "Closed system" mentality, leading to increased vulnerability
- Lack of fulfillment and a sense of being appreciated, leading to a sense of disillusionment among employees and a lack of loyalty
- Depletion of resources

The **Center** direction puts our focus on:
- Developing the business's leadership
- Looking at the big picture and assessing the long-term consequences of our actions and decisions
- Actively guiding the growth and evolution of the business

This focus helps us avoid these common business problems:
- Lack of leadership; inadequate management team
- Doing business in such a way that there is a negative impact on external environment leading to negative PR within community and/or intervention by EPA, SEC, etc.
- Not anticipating/seeing changes in marketplace, technology, etc.; being blindsided or outmaneuvered by

- something in the external environment
- Premature expansion; uncontrolled growth with inadequate cash flow
- Loss of focus: What business are we in?

The Adaptability of the Circle

As we learned in Chapter 2, we can use the Circle to address many business issues and problems because its innate gifts that can help us in many ways.

The Circle's Gifts: What the Circle Can Help Us Do

- Create and maintain good Relationships
- Generate Movement
- Get in touch with what is True
- Create and Maintain Boundaries
- Attain Clarity
- Maintain Neutrality
- Focus our Attention
- Hold an Altruistic Agenda
- Gain Sense of Direction
- Bridge and Translate between entities
- Practice Moderation and Balance
- Practice Humility
- Embrace Sharing
- Practice Equitable Exchange
- Create effective Structures
- Learn from the Past
- Grow & Evolve Our Business (and ourselves)
- Find Unity in Diversity
- Consider More of the Whole
- Connect with the Sacred

The Circle is also endlessly adaptable. The Circle can help us organize, address, and work through all of the tasks and challenges involved in building, running, or evolving a business. No matter what we need to accomplish, we can create a "custom" Circle blueprint to help us address it. On the next pages are just a few examples. (These and many more will be described in detail in Volume 2, The Circle Resource Book):

~ Business Revolution through Ancestral Wisdom~

Example 1: Envisioning your business

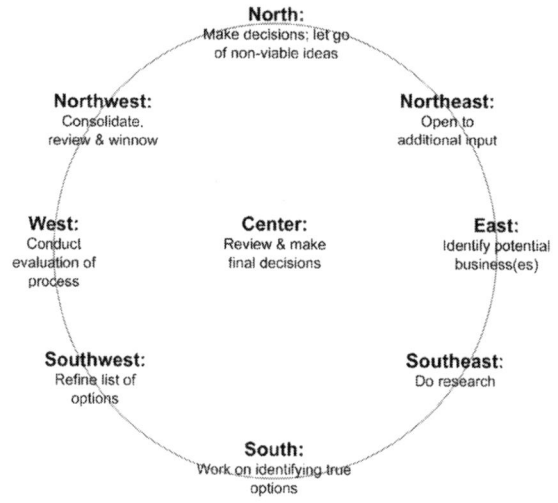

- **North:** Make decisions; let go of non-viable ideas
- **Northwest:** Consolidate, review & winnow
- **Northeast:** Open to additional input
- **West:** Conduct evaluation of process
- **Center:** Review & make final decisions
- **East:** Identify potential business(es)
- **Southwest:** Refine list of options
- **Southeast:** Do research
- **South:** Work on identifying true options

Example 2: Establishing your business's external imagery

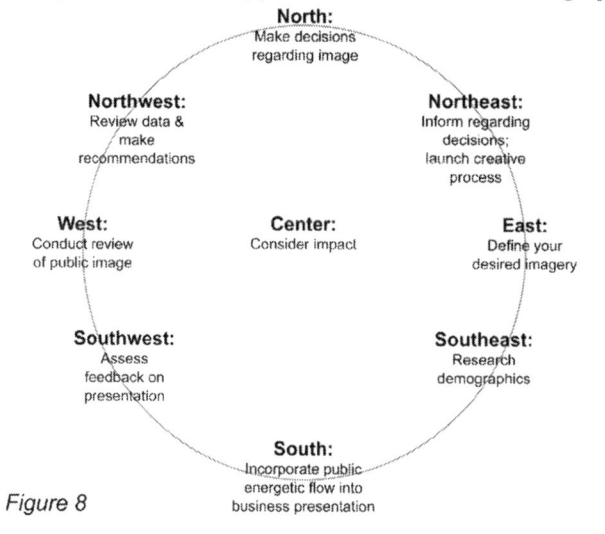

- **North:** Make decisions regarding image
- **Northwest:** Review data & make recommendations
- **Northeast:** Inform regarding decisions; launch creative process
- **West:** Conduct review of public image
- **Center:** Consider impact
- **East:** Define your desired imagery
- **Southwest:** Assess feedback on presentation
- **Southeast:** Research demographics
- **South:** Incorporate public energetic flow into business presentation

Figure 8

Example 3: Designing information flow into your business

North: Spiritual perspective

Northwest: Employee feedback

Northeast: All other necessary data

West: Internal evaluation

Center: Long-term implications

East: Inspiration & vision

Southwest: Feedback loops & resolution processes

Southeast: Practical information

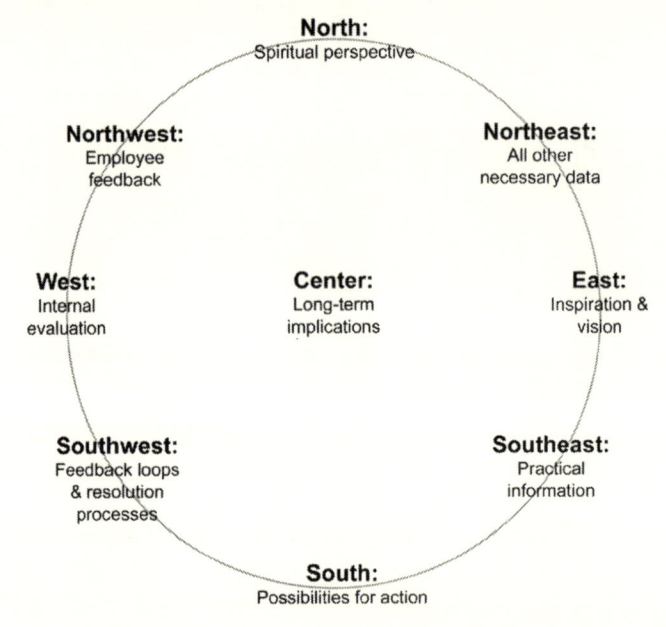

South: Possibilities for action

Figure 8b

The Benefits of Using the Circle as our Primary Business Blueprint

There are many benefits to be gained from adopting the Circle as the primary blueprint for a business. Here are a few.

- **The Circle will Increase our Ability to Deal with Complexity**

All businesses are made up of multiple inter-relationships. Therefore, you need a tool that can help you deal with complex input. The Circle is such a tool. The Circle's continuous movement enables it to be in touch with everything. Its innate holistic nature can help us take many different kinds of people and perspectives into consideration. It is robust enough to help us to address the whole range of human issues, from questions of ideological perspective to logistical tasks, to human resource and productivity issues.

Dealing with complex issues requires us to hold focus, and stay in neutrality until the best solution is found. We need to come to clarity, find direction, create appropriate structure, and set appropriate boundaries. As we've discussed, the Circle has all those abilities as part of its nature—and more. The Universal Laws and Principles and the Rights of All Beings, which are innate to the Circle, expand our capacity to find our way through complex situations while maintaining our impartiality. In particular, our ability to give all of the stakeholders (and their ideas), the Right to Be will assist us in maintaining neutrality.

- **The Circle will Increase our Ability to Address Problems Successfully**

Because the Circle is always in movement, there is always an energetic flow. Imagine a millwheel, continuously lifting water from a stream. In the same way, the Circle continuously gathers in new information. This ensures that the knowledge available for problem-solving is constantly being refreshed and replenished, and that new options are always being gathered.

In addition, issues and problems are often inter-related. The Circle can help us address these kinds of challenges because it is masterful with relationships. If an issue is multi-dimensional, we might need to break it down into its constituent parts, while also retaining cohesiveness and inter-flow between the parts. The Circle can help us do this. When we need to resolve a multi-leveled issue or problem the Circle blueprint has the advantage because many circles can relate to and interact with each other simultaneously (as in a Spiral). Linear thinking can help us break the issues down, but it can't help with keeping them related. We'll discuss this further in Volume 2.

Another way that the Circle helps with problem-solving lies in the fact that the Circle naturally promotes balance. Thus, the solutions that arise will be aimed at promoting balance and clarity on the subject matter. Because the Circle is always relating to everything around it, no matter how complex the problem, there is a circle format that can address it (as we'll demonstrate in Volume 2). In sum, the Circle presents a path to deal with modern perspectives and complex issues, while giving valuable advice about situations that we would struggle to untangle, let alone solve, if we relied only on our human skills and abilities.

• The Circle Will Increase Our Capacity to Deal with Change

We humans have created an energetic dynamic on a global level wherein things change very quickly. As we've said, human beings are uncomfortable with change, and we are even more uncomfortable with constant, rapid change. Unfortunately, that's exactly what we have set in motion. Unless we find a way to become more comfortable with change, we will find it increasingly difficult to cope with the world. We need a tool that can help us contend with change.

Change is a Universal Law. The Circle has no prejudice towards change because it has no emotional investments in a given situation. Therefore, the Circle is a great tool to help us deal with change.[18]

• The Circle Can Help Us Realize Abundant Return on our Efforts

~ Business Revolution through Ancestral Wisdom~

In the linear pattern we tend to have expectations of immediate gain on any energy we expend. We are often disappointed. This is because the line actually consumes energy, and has no capacity to give back. It can only take us from one prospective source of energy to another.

In contrast, the energy in a circle is self-renewing. This means that, when we truly engage wholeheartedly with the Circle, all the energy that we put into our efforts will *never be lost*, and will *come back to us in full measure, in due time*.

This means that when we put energy into a Circle, it not only doesn't dissipate, it grows. So, the rewards will be greater, just not so immediate. We will have to learn patience, and to practice accepting that the harvest comes in the fullness of time, in accordance with the laws of the Universe—not at our whim. This is a more indirect, but significantly more rewarding way to conduct our businesses and our lives.

In return for all its gifts, the Circle will ask more of us. It will:

- Ask us to become more conscious, particularly in the beginning stages of anything we do. We will find this challenging. This is <u>not</u> a limitation of the Circle, but a fact about human beings. The Circle also asks us to be patient. It will take time and practice to set up a new blueprint. We will have to learn to hold off on expecting fast returns on our efforts, which will be frustrating at first. The benefits are great. Guided by the Circle, our efforts will yield more in the long run, as they will be in alignment with Universal Flow.

- Prod us to be more flexible, to accept more of the whole, to encompass many different kinds of people and perspectives, while giving them all the Right to Be. Sometimes that can be overwhelming and challenging to humans.
- Ask us to take others into consideration, and to seek effective compromises.

- Ask us to let go of our illusions and emotional investments in things. The Circle will continuously present us with what is true, from a Universal perspective. This may catch us by surprise, and trigger our resistance, which is normal. Once we become aware of it, we can move toward it, give it the Right to Be, and finally accept it. The Universal Principle of Acceptance is key to moving through our resistance.

- Often remind us that we are not the pinnacle of creation, privileged above all. It will also remind us that we are not in control. Because we are insecure, we want to be special, and dominate. The linear pattern feeds our illusions. Adopting the Circle requires letting go of the belief that we are more important than other aspects of the Universe. Adopting the Circle requires true humility, and acknowledging we are part of the whole. This will challenge us.

The Circle's Effects on Human Beings

As we said in the first chapter, the line interacts with many of our human factors to bring about a business climate that is actually quite harsh and unsettling for us. Because humans are insecure, we often try to control things, circumstances, and people, thinking this will help make sure we get what we need and want. The line promises control, and immediate gratification. It's the pattern for aggressive, forward action. So, by its nature, the line supports our being extremist and aggressive to achieve our ends. It creates and reinforces an excessively "macho" business culture. In this way, we unconsciously perpetuate aggressive, uncomfortable work environments that continuously trigger our insecurity.

Compounding that, linear thinking distances us from the consequences of our actions. It encourages short-term thinking, which is not optimal. The business literature has called this to our attention, but it's extremely difficult to change in practice. This is because the linear pattern makes it virtually impossible for us to see—let alone connect with—the long-term, big picture. Picture in your mind's eye that you are walking along a line, and you want to consider the past before taking your next step. Notice that you can only turn and look straight back. Only the recent past is in your line of vision. Your view to anything further back is obstructed by what is directly behind you. This makes it problematic to learn from the past. We even forget our history. Now, still walking along the line, look forward toward the future. Notice that you can only see what's directly in front of you, in the near-term. Beyond that, your vision drops off precipitously.

The line restricts our ability to see the whole picture. Not only does that make it hard for us to learn from history, it also gives us little sense of completion or fulfillment. Without a sense of the whole, our actions tend to be piecemeal and lacking in a larger sense of meaning. We do one thing after another without a clear sense of where we're going, or whether we're actually making progress. The line also explains why we are driven to consume resources (both non-human and human), without attention to conserving or giving back. In brief, the great unexamined consequence of linearity is that it deludes us into thinking it's the path to happiness, but it's inherently incapable of fulfilling its promise.

In contrast, the Circle will help us manage our innate insecurity, and mitigate our inherent tendency to extremism. The Circle supports people finding balance and moderation. The Circle enables us to have 360° vision, thus giving us a much better sense of the whole of an issue, problem, or organization. Because the Circle is a continuous process—evolving into a spiral—it organically and continuously connects the present with the past and future. In this way, it encourages and supports long-term, big picture thinking.

In addition, the application of the Universal Laws and Principles and the Rights of Beingness, which are inherent in the Circle, supports us to pay attention to self-management and inner alignment. In this way, the Circle supports the development of mature qualities such as patience, tolerance, and discipline. By making the commitment to allow the Universal Law of Altruism (doing that which is best for all concerned, including oneself) to guide us, we consider what is best for the Whole, not just for ourselves. The Principle of Humility encourages us to be supportive, tolerant, and accepting of both others and ourselves. Rather than striving for the appearance of perfection (which is unattainable), the Circle encourages mature creative expression. When the Rights of All Beings are practiced, we can use mistakes as opportunities for learning. This fosters generative thinking; we are less defensive and more open, which leads to greater clarity.

The Circle opens the door for these important values and qualities to be re-introduced into the business world. It fosters their flowering, since they are no longer perceived to be in conflict with the way in which business is conducted. Rather than pursuing amusement or the illusion of fulfillment, this supports humans in finding fulfillment in their work lives. This will have a profoundly positive effect on human beings, and on all involved, including the environment.

--Effects on Human Beings—

Current Linear pattern:	Circle-based Format:
- Triggers our innate insecurity	- Helps us manage our innate insecurity
- Fosters extremism	- Mitigates our tendency toward extremism
- Supports aggression and assertiveness	- Supports moderation and balance
- Narrows our focus, which promotes individual achievement, looking out for self and one's own	- Enables us to take a wider perspective, see more of the whole picture

Current Linear pattern:	Circle-based Format:
Encourages the illusion of control and the instrumental use of others from a self-serving place	Encourages cooperation with others, a willingness to compromise and to be supportive and compassionate
Encourages selfish motivations, including self-sacrifice and martyrism as extreme self-centered responses	Encourages use of Universal Laws and Principles and the Rights of All Beings to guide actions, particularly the Law of Altruism: doing that which is best for all concerned, including one's self
Emphasizes perfection; little toleration for mistakes	Supports our viewing mistakes as opportunities for learning, so we honor them
Encourages immediate gratification and short-term thinking	Encourages us to look at the big picture and consider the long-term effects of our actions
Encourages consumption as a marker of success and/or replacement for fulfillment	Supports true fulfillment and long-lasting prosperity through sharing and the gratitude that is returned because of one's caring actions

Like all the other blueprints, the Circle has some characteristics that we might think of as limitations. We need to be aware of these as well, so that we truly understand how to best use the Circle.

Limitations of the Circle Blueprint

The Circle can help us encompass many different perspectives. This is a tremendous advantage in our complex world. It can help us find solutions through compromise. There are some trade-offs, however. One trade-off is that the Circle's energetic profile is less aggressive than the line (initially). The Circle is certainly capable of generating aggressive movement, but this requires unified energy—which takes a while to consolidate. Once that energy is consolidated, it's powerful and much easier for us to adapt to. Whereas the energy generated by the line is sharp and aggressive, Circle energy is a steady force. It's like the difference between a wind sheer and a strong, consistent 25 mph wind.

Another trade-off is that the pull toward compromise may mean that some people will tend to concede excessively, putting their self-identity at risk. When working with the Circle, we need to be mindful of this human tendency to take compromise to an extreme.

Sometimes, we see the Circle as more limited than it is. This is because of the biases inherent in linear thinking itself. We've tended to associate the Circle with simpler, more "primitive" cultures. This leads us to underestimate the sophistication of the Circle and dismiss it, rather than explore its full potential. We've also tended to see the Circle as feminine. The truth is that the Circle is gender-neutral.

These are the primary limitations of the Circle. Hopefully, you can see that they are more perceived than real, and that they are also connected to great benefits. The actual limitations lie more in our humanness than in the Circle. Fortunately, the Circle supports us in managing our human factors, whereas the linear pattern intensifies them.

It's important to understand how the line and the Circle compare as the foundational structure for business. To make an informed choice, we need to take into consideration the benefits and limitations of each. Below is a detailed comparison.

~ Business Revolution through Ancestral Wisdom ~

--Comparison of Line and Circle as Blueprints--

Line:	Circle:
- Is a partial blueprint	- Is a whole and complete universal blueprint
- Is a tool invented by humans that humans can control	- Is intrinsic and natural to organic beings; is not a human invention and cannot be controlled by humans
- Reinforces putting humans (and their comfort) first and foremost	- Supports everything, equally; does not put humans first
- Supports the illusion of control	- Reminds us that we are not the pinnacle of creation and control is an illusion
- Movement not intrinsic; relies on brute force	- Movement is intrinsic
- Supports aggression to achieve our ends	- Depends on unified energy for aggressive movement
- Facilitates speedy results; very efficient, for short spurts; encourages immediate gratification and short-term thinking	- More time-consuming to set up; return on efforts takes longer, but exceptionally efficient over long haul; encourages patience

~ Business Revolution through Ancestral Wisdom ~

Line:	Circle:
- So stable and rigid that it has difficulty keeping a constant flow of energy	- Energy flow is constant, paced, and moderate
- Energy deteriorates	- Energy is self-renewing
- To continue trajectory, energy must be obtained from elsewhere; promotes consumption	- Does not consume, but maintains and amplifies all energy put into it; promotes energy conservation
- Needs constant maintenance	- Requires little or no maintenance
- Supports narrowing down focus to one subject at a time, for a short time (can't hold energy, so can't hold the clarity for any length of time)	- Fosters clarity and the ability to look at things from multiple perspectives for an infinite period of time (because of access to Universal Flow, which is infinite)
- Narrow perspective increases ability to specialize, analyze, and take things apart	- Innately holistic, integrating, and comprehensive; facilitates wholeness
- Capable of supporting consistency, but only with one aspect at a time	- Fosters consistency in all aspects (brings in all of the parts)
- Can rely mental energy to force consistency, bully, and dominate	- Does not rely solely on mental energy; doesn't foster force or domination

~ Business Revolution through Ancestral Wisdom~

Line:	**Circle:**
- Can be contradictory in its processes; can lead to be short-sighted and overly critical with no practical feedback or solutions	- Asks us to be conscious, and willing to relinquish the illusion of control.
- Can define and hold boundary, but only for short time	- Can define and hold a boundary indefinitely
- Equality is not inherent; encourages instrumental use of others from a self-serving place	- Equality is inherent; encourages working with others from a place of wholeness
- Can help create and support great wealth and/or fame, for a limited amount of time, but at great cost	- Supports us in discovering what works best for all concerned, including ourselves, over the long-term; supports finding solutions through compromise
- Leaves us open to illusion and delusion, prejudice and righteousness	- Presents what is true, and asks us to acknowledge what is real
- Mistakes tend to be repeated, yet little toleration for mistakes	- Facilitates learning from past; mistakes and failures are opportunities for growth
- Supports spurts of creativity; drives certain, select efforts forward; can lead to tremendous discoveries	- Puts us in touch with an infinite source of creative energy

~ Business Revolution through Ancestral Wisdom ~

Line:	Circle:
• Obstructs perception of the whole which limits flexibility	• Exceedingly flexible, accepting, and encompassing of many different kinds of modalities (can sometimes be overwhelming to humans)
• Supports limited creativity and flexibility, so adaptive change does not come easily	• True growth and evolution are inherent, so fosters adaptive change
• Can support rapid transitions, but only in one area at a time	• Supports moderate, consistent transitions by encompassing and integrating as it goes. Nothing is left behind
• Singular focus limits ability to support large-scale transformation	• Innately transformational; can support harmonious transformation of entire system
• Reinforces use of combative force; can be used to create and support personal power, as well as the abuse of it	• Does not support use of undue force or seduction to compel an energy to do something against its will; supports free will and choice
• Fosters creating experiences and environments that are harsh and disorienting to human beings, i.e., "macho" business culture	• Helps us create harmonious, productive environments

Line:	Circle:
• Leads to mindless over-consumption of resources without attention to giving back	• Supports consideration of all concerned, looking at big picture and long-term effects, and replenishment of resources
• Exacerbates our human factors; triggers our innate insecurity and fosters extremism	• Helps us manage our human factors by fostering moderation and balance; supports us to align with Universal Flow and to live in accordance with Universal Laws and Principles and the Rights of All Beings

In this chapter we discussed the many gifts the Circle can bring to business, and to us as human beings. Even the Circle's perceived limitations can act as boundaries, and be blessings in reality.

In case you're concerned that adopting the Circle means giving up the line entirely, rest assured that is not the case. By its nature, the Circle blueprint is exceedingly flexible and accepting. It is encompassing of many different kinds of modalities, including the line. The Circle can relate to and include the line. As we see in geometry, any circle can contain an infinite number of lines. Therefore, if we use the Circle as our primary blueprint, we can also use the line as needed. This gives us the best of both worlds. When the line is contained within the Circle, its effectiveness is enhanced. When we employ linear thinking strategically, within the larger context of the Circle, we develop a way of thinking that is efficient, flexible, and much less susceptible to illusion than linear thinking alone. We are more able to see what is really there, and to accept it. There is greater depth and breadth to our understanding.

The Circle is a practical tool, and more. It can put us in touch with an infinite source of support that is available for our evolution and growth, so that we become part of something larger than ourselves. No doubt this description sounds too idyllic to be true, but we submit that the Circle is a powerful construct whose potential in the modern world has yet to be fully explored.

Chapter Nine
The Circle:
A Bridge to Transformation

The world is becoming unified through a process we know as "globalization." Our world is being transformed because business is in the midst of an evolutionary process. Where once a business's influence was generally limited to its immediate surroundings, now any business has the potential to influence anything, anywhere in the world.

Globalization is a vast transition, penetrating into every corner of the world. Business is the agent behind this process of unification of the world. It's also the chief guide and overseer, and herein lies the problem—and the opening.

As many critics are pointing out, this transition seems to be taking place in a way that benefits the few at the expense of the many. It's occurring in a way that does not support the well-being of all the people on the Earth, let alone the Earth itself and other species. In fact, it's often disruptive, even wrenching, and potentially disastrous for many.[19] In other words, it's not happening in accordance with the Universal Law of Altruism. As visionary environmentalist and entrepreneur Paul Hawken writes in his most recent book, *Blessed Unrest*: "Globalization began just over five hundred years ago when Western Europeans began to accept the idea that the earth is round, something Indian and Chinese civilizations already knew. Ever since then, in myriad ways, commerce, armies, travelers, and scholars have worked toward integrating human activity with geography, encircling the globe with development that arose from Western appetite."[20]

Why is this so? Some would say, "That's just the way business is." We disagree. It's not due to the nature of business *per se*, but because of the partial blueprint that underlies and shapes it. Globalization, like most business activities, is being carried out on the basis of the line. As the foundation for a major, worldwide transition, the line has significant and severe limitations. The line can be an appropriate pattern for a rapid transition that is simple and straightforward, where only one dimension needs to change. Globalization, however, is vast, complex, and multi-dimensional. The linear construct is inadequate to the task. It pays little heed to—and often operates at the expense of—all the other things around it: the global workforce, children and families, communities, the environment, et al. The linear pattern is not robust enough to support business to bring about this transition. It's too limited to support business to do that which is best for all concerned, including itself. (In other words, the line is too limited to enable business to operate in accordance with the Law of Altruism.) That's why the benefits of globalization are so narrow, and the negative effects so widespread.

Part of the problem is that our unconscious over-use of the linear pattern has caused us to misperceive the true nature and potential of business. Business is one of the ways that Universal Energy can manifest in the physical world. Universal Energy always flows in a way that creates the greatest benefit for all concerned, and supports the continuous evolution of the whole. From the perspective of Universal Flow, then, the purpose of business is to *provide equitable exchange and change life conditions for better* of all concerned. Business is not a realm separate from the rest of life, with its own rules; it's an energetic agent for the enhancement, improvement, and fulfillment of the lives of all, without prejudice.

~ Business Revolution through Ancestral Wisdom ~

Business has the potential to unify the world, and to bring benefits to everyone. This is the true purpose and the seed of potential that lies within business. Business has the power to connect people, communities, governments, and countries into a unified whole. This power bestows on it the capacity to enable us live in peaceful coexistence with each other, and with the Earth. We know that business has the ability to connect the world because it's *already doing so*, just in a very incomplete and unfulfilling way. Business is failing to live up to its true, full potential. It represents a vast stream of blocked energy waiting to be tapped.

We are at a major point in human history. One option is to continue to use the line as the underlying pattern shaping globalization, and to reconcile ourselves to the consequences. Ultimately, that is counter-productive, for if we restrict the benefits of globalization to the few, we constrict our prospective markets, diminish our capacity to manifest, and reduce our prospective profits and benefits. Another option is to attempt to halt or control the process of globalization. Many concerned people favor this option, despite the obstacles. A third possibility is that we consider using the Circle blueprint to support the transition to globalization. At this moment, the world is poised—we have only to decide which way to go.

A Universal Perspective

To help us make our decision, we need to understand globalization from a universal perspective. It is actually a byproduct of a much larger process: the ongoing evolution of humanity. Business is a human creation, and an artifact of our ongoing, evolutionary process.

As we discussed previously, Evolution is one of the Universal Laws and Principles. Evolution applies to everything. Seen from this perspective, the ongoing evolution of business is inevitable, and globalization is a natural outgrowth of the evolutionary process. However, the *form* that globalization is taking is human-created. We humans push the limits of our ability to influence, control, and dominate things; and we use the linear pattern to do so. This is the case with globalization.

What is the proper response, from a universal perspective? From a universal perspective, we cannot and should not attempt to control, dominate, or stop the evolution of business. We cannot and should not attempt to block the transition of business from local to global, as that is already in process. But, as humans, we have the ability, and the responsibility, to direct and support this transition so it can occur in accordance with Universal Flow, *i.e.,* in accordance with the Law of Altruism, to the greater benefit of all. The Circle can help.

In times of transition, we must build bridges. Humans can direct and support transitions by creating links that enable energy to flow from where we are now, to where we want to go. We must now create those bridges to direct the flow of globalization in the direction of altruism. We can use the Circle to build that bridgework. It has the depth and capability to serve the practical needs of business, while also keeping us in alignment with Universal Flow. It can support harmonious and multi-dimensional change.

The challenge could not be more formidable, nor the obstacles greater. The Circle is a lot like David's slingshot when he set out to defeat Goliath. It appears inadequate to the task. And yet, as Paul Hawken presciently wrote, to "globalize" literally means to "make something round."[21] It's time that we embraced the true meaning of globalization and welcomed the Circle back into the world.

If we walk the path laid out the by the Circle, that path will lead us into a different paradigm for business. Many of us have been longing for one that is both practical and nurturing of the human spirit. If we begin to use the Circle as the blueprint for business, then this desirable transformation is inevitable. As the ancients knew, when we walk the path of the Circle it lifts to a Spiral: the symbol—and very structure—of evolution itself. That is why we propose the Circle as the shape of our possible future.

A New Sense of Purpose for Business

In our current, linear-based format, the purpose of business is singular: to make money. There is room for little else in the domain of purpose. Today's businesses are pressured to focus narrowly on generating wealth for a few stakeholders, as quickly as possible. Outside of that narrow focus, there is resistance to being answerable for the consequences. As a general rule, business lobbies against laws that attempt to hold it accountable and takes little responsibility for deleterious effects on the environment, communities, employees, or even customers unless external pressure is applied.

From the perspective of Universal Flow, however, the true purpose of business is to *change life conditions for the better, and to conduct itself in a way that benefits all concerned, including the business itself.* It follows, then, that the goal of any specific business is twofold:

- *To fulfill people's needs and, secondarily, their wants*
- *To effectively and efficiently do this within the larger context of the Universal Rights of All Beings and Universal Laws and Principles*

This sets a new standard. It broadens the focus of business. It allows business to reclaim its true value, which is creating a comfortable co-existence for all, while maintaining standards of behavior that take into consideration humans, nature, all other species, and the Earth itself.

A Different Relationship to the Earth and its Resources

Linearity is inherently separating. Consequentially, business is seen as separate from the rest of life. This mindset facilitates our leeching energy and resources from the natural world, our personal lives, and our families at an alarming rate to further the interests of business. Little attention is paid to the replenishment and renewal of these resources. There's not much priority put on sustainability, or looking at the big picture. Resources—including humans—are seen as consumable. These are all symptoms of linear thinking, which makes it difficult to think or act more holistically. The linear pattern forces its will on the environment, often at the expense of human beings, other creatures, the Earth, or even the truth.

In the Circle format, all resources are seen as sacred because they are all manifestations of Universal Energy. The focus is on honoring, renewing, and recycling. The Circle sees business as integrated with life. There is no separation. The Circle recognizes that business has both spiritual and material dimensions, and even more importantly, it fosters and supports the integration of those dimensions. [22]

A Healthier, More Supportive, and Effective Business Climate

The line is the blueprint for aggressive speed, and it narrows our vision so we can focus on the target. These are the defining characteristics of the business world: Faster is better, no matter the cost to humans, other creatures or the Earth. We all want instant satisfaction, immediate results, and return on investment in the short-term. We pay little attention to the future, or to the long-term effects or ramifications of our actions. We want "bigger," and "more," and to be "super-sized." "Growth" is defined by size alone, and it's an unquestioned imperative. Because of the line's aggressive nature—and our extremist tendencies—we get swept up in the game. In fact, it has recently been said that big business is meeting all the diagnostic criteria for being designated a sociopath.[23] We have created a "winner take all" context in which mistakes and failures are not easily tolerated. We do this despite the actual fact that mistakes and failures are the most important sources of learning we have. We have a "learning disability," an inability to learn from the past.[24] In a world that is constantly changing, there is little sense of continuity, and little reason to hold onto old-fashioned moralities. Numbers can be manipulated to tell a favorable story; facts can be maneuvered to support pre-defined ends. Competition is seen as a threat and a problem to be disposed of; you want to intimidate, consume, or bury your competition. It's thought normal to aspire to power, without any guidance as to its proper obtainment or use.

If we learn to embrace the Circle, we can begin to turn this around—quite literally. With the Circle, the present and future are equally important. One is not sacrificed for the other. When decisions need to be made, their long-term effects on all concerned are deliberately considered, and the Law of Altruism holds sway. The Circle supports us in building a strong foundation at the very beginning so that integrity, longevity, and sustainability are at the core of the business. The Circle fosters thinking about the good of the whole. The focus is on cooperating with the flow of Universal Energy in order to benefit all, with no losers. Because the Circle has the Universal Guidelines built into its very nature, it will help us create mutually beneficial energetic exchanges as our primary way of relating to one another.

Where the linear pattern leads toward compartmentalization, the Circle format puts great importance on understanding the *complete reality of a situation* in order to inform appropriate action. There is always an emphasis on discovering *what truly works, i.e.,* what works well and benefits all concerned. This helps us cut through our illusions and delusions. And, as our fantasy drops away, we also have a better understanding of what true power is (as distinct from brute force). In time, this should help us develop greater discretion with regard to the use of power and force.

With the Circle, your relationship to competition changes. You support your competition's Right to Be, and allow for healthy competition that fosters continuous improvement.

A New Definition of Personal Success

Today, success in business is defined as material gain: the more wealth, the better. The focus is on individual achievement, which is frequently defined as winning over others. As the bumper sticker puts it, "The one with the most toys wins." In a very real sense, we are people lacking a sense of direction, working for organizations that also lack a sense of direction. We're endlessly repeating patterns that do not bring us real happiness, while amusing ourselves with high-tech toys, entertainments, and other distractions.

In the realm of Universal Flow and the Circle, however, success is something altogether different. Personal wealth and recognition are not goals that we pursue directly. These things can still be achieved, but—and this is key—they are *byproducts.* They are the *rewards that come about as a natural result of fulfilling the true purpose of business.*

And now let us say a bit more about what success really is. Financial gain or material wealth is only one facet of true success. It's success only in the South direction. So, if a businessperson stops there, he or she has only achieved success in a very limited, narrow, and immature sense. A businessperson is truly successful only if he or she transits the entire Circle, successfully negotiating the tasks set forth in each direction. According to the Circle, a truly successful businessperson is one who:

- Is open to new ideas, and can articulate a clear vision (East)
- Researches, plans for, and attains the resources necessary for success—including honestly evaluating his or her own strengths and weaknesses in that regard (SE)
- Brings a business into manifestation (South)
- Actively seeks feedback; continuously adjusts (SW)
- Reflects upon and evaluates his or her "success" in terms of its effects on all concerned, *i.e.,* in light of the Universal Law of Altruism (West)
- Seeks to create greater balance in the workplace and in his or her own life (NW)
- Asks for wisdom to help guide decisions; is able to make commitments and to release that which no longer serves; acts as an exemplar for others (N)
- Shares abundance with those who have contributed to personal and business success, including the larger community; passes wisdom along to others (NE)

- Looks at the long-term effects of his/her actions on the world, the Earth itself, and future generations; reaps the satisfaction of a life well-lived (Center)

If we begin to walk the path laid out by the Circle, the path will lead us into a different paradigm for business. It is a path that unites the practical and sacred. It is a path that is nurturing of the human spirit, as well as functional and effective in helping us address real human needs. We need not fear that we cannot make the change because the Circle path will lift to a Spiral, the very structure of evolution itself. Beneficial growth is inherent and inevitable. The Circle can help us to transform the world of business, bringing it into alignment with Universal Flow. This is a transformation we are longing for.

And so let us begin, deliberately, incrementally, a step at a time. In keeping with what we have learned from the Circle, we can proceed in moderation, remembering that a great transformation is actually made up of many small transitions. We need not race to abandon the line, but rather strive to choose more consciously and deliberately the blueprint that is most appropriate to the need. That is the way of the Circle.

--Comparison of Blueprints and Resulting Business Climate –

- Linear Approach -	- Circle Approach -
The Purpose of Business is:	
• To make money; material gain, particularly for stockholders and individuals	• To fulfill people's needs and, secondarily, their wants effectively and efficiently within the larger context of Universal Laws and Principles and the Universal Rights of Beingness
	• To be an agent of the evolution of the Whole

- Linear Approach -

Values Promoted:
- Speed; quick return on investment, quick success
- Bigger and more are inherently better
- Looking good; perfection and the appearance of perfection
- Winning over others; Individual achievement
- Needing to be right

Priorities:
- Direct pursuit of material wealth and recognition
- Growing the business (measured as increase in size, revenues, etc.)

View of Resources:
- Resources are consumable; replenishment is not priority

View of Competition:
- Competition is a problem to be eliminated

- Circle Approach -

- Integrity, longevity, sustainability
- Doing that which works best for all concerned, including self
- Discovering what works well to benefit all concerned
- Acknowledging and accepting the truth of situations; continuously learning and improving upon the past
- Equitable, mutually beneficial exchange

- Cooperating with the flow of Universal Energy to benefit all; material wealth and recognition are byproducts
- Evolving the business along a path of true, beneficial growth

- All resources are sacred; high priority on honoring, renewing, recycling resources

- Competition is beneficial

Relationship to Time:

- Linear Approach -
- Focused on short-term; seeks immediate results or ROI
- Somewhat future-oriented, but only in a vague sense

- Circle Approach -
- Satisfaction is obtained as a byproduct of work well done, in whatever time it takes
- Both present and future-oriented; concerned with long-term effects of actions

Relationship to Truth:

- Susceptible to illusion and delusion (what we want to be true vs. what *is* true)
- In worse case, facts can be manipulated to support pre-defined ends: "spin-doctoring"

- High importance placed on understanding the complete reality of a situation in order to inform appropriate action

Relationship to Power:

- Linear Approach -
- Focus on forcing things to happen in accordance with our wants and timetables
- True power confused with brute force

- Circle Approach -
- Supports free will and choice, does not support use of undue force or seduction to compel an energy to do something against its will
- Helps us distinguish true power from false (*i.e.*, brute force); fosters discretion with regard to use of power

- Linear Approach -

View of Success:
- Narrow: defined as financial gain and/or fame

Relationship of Business to Life:
- Business separated from the rest of life; business has its own rules

- Fosters compartmentalization versus acknowledgement of whole

- Circle Approach -

- Expansive; Success is well-rounded, holistic, involving entire Circle

- Business integrated with life

- Fosters thinking about the good of the Whole

Appendix
Circle Templates for Business

Compassion Help Circle

Because there is both a Universal and human aspect to compassion, we often need help determining how best to act. We can turn to the Circle.

On the following pages we describe a Circle process we can use to help us gain perspective on a situation. It will help us find a course of action that is both well-balanced and compassionate.

Appendix

Compassion Help Circle

North: Implement action

Northeast: Get feedback

East: Go back to origin

Southeast: Gather information

South: Work toward resolution

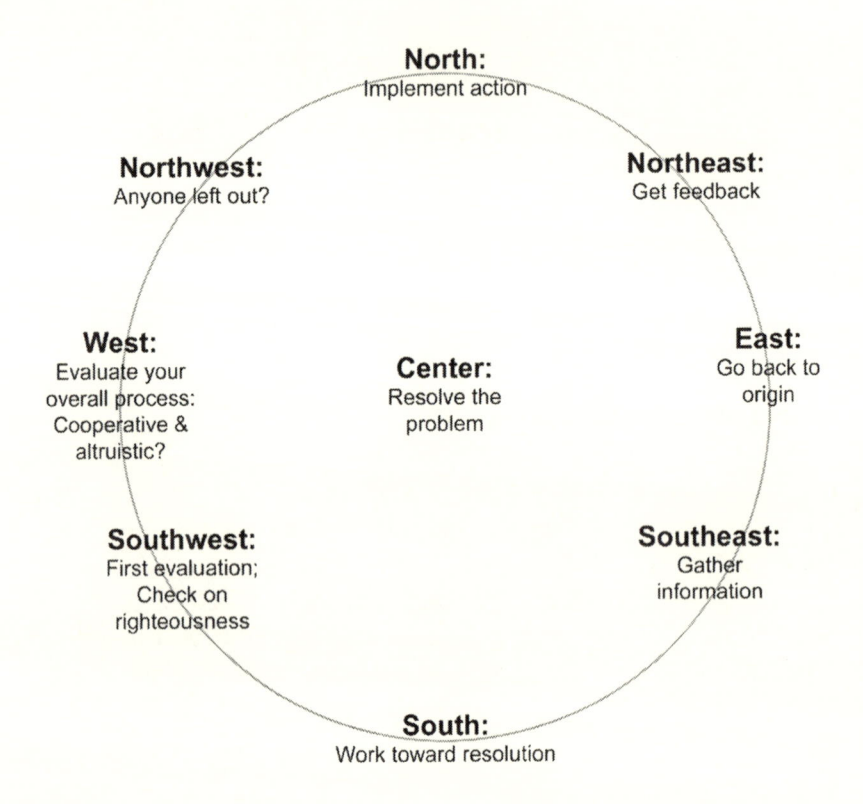

Southwest: First evaluation; Check on righteousness

West: Evaluate your overall process: Cooperative & altruistic?

Northwest: Anyone left out?

Center: Resolve the problem

Figure 9

The Compassion Help Circle is the Circle's perspective on how to hold an energy that is both well-balanced and compassionate on a subject matter. Here is the process to follow:

East: Go back to the Origin - When an issue of this nature arises, you may find yourself in a state of confusion, and your emotions may be involved. This step will help you gain a sense of

~ 202 ~

perspective and help you regain focus.

Your goal at this step is to assess the overall importance of the issue. Turn your thoughts to the original participants and subject matter. Ask yourself the following questions:

- Who were the original participants in the situation?
- How important is this issue in the general picture of the business, the department, or the subject matter?

Southeast: Gather Information - Now, collect all known information about the subject and people involved. This includes information you don't want to hear. Just accumulate it; refrain from making any assumptions or judgments.

South: Work Toward Resolution - Start by looking at all the information you gathered. Work on accepting it, and trying to come to a solution/resolution about it.

The purpose of this step is to "clean house" (emotionally speaking) so that you can look at the data logically. Unless you do that, your emotions will lead you to jump to conclusions.

Southwest: First evaluation: Check on righteousness - Now, look at the work you did in the South, and ask yourself:

- How did I do with the information? Have I done this work without prejudice? Without judgment or righteousness?

This is where the Circle is particularly good at keeping us on track. It helps us to gently but firmly get our human factors out of the mix.

West: Evaluate your overall process - Step back and look at your overall process so far, assessing whether you've proceeded in accordance with Universal Laws and Principles. Did you do it cooperatively? Was there cooperative energy involved in your process? Altruistic energy? Here, you evaluate (and, hopefully, validate), your process in a way that's gentle but firm.

Northwest: Anyone left out? - Before you implement any action, double-check yourself. Make sure that no one who is essential to resolution has been left out of loop. Make sure that things haven't become confused, and that you're dealing with the same subject matter you defined in the East.

North: Implement action - This is where you do something about the subject matter with understanding and care. You implement a solution based on the process you've gone through so far.

Northeast: Get feedback - Once you've implemented, you look at the consequences. You gauge everyone's reactions. If feedback tells you that you need to reconsider your action, then go back around and double-check everything again.

Center: Resolve the problem - Once you're satisfied that you've done your best, and that the resolution you've come to is the best you can do, then proceed to the Center. Here, you come to a place of true acceptance about everything you did, and how you chose to resolve the problem. "OK," you say to yourself, "This is the way it has to be." Give your resolution the Right to Be. This creates a sense of completion and peace.

East: Begin a new cycle.

Example: Establishing a Foundation for Self-Employment

Self-employment is an important expression of one's being. It's a commitment to yourself as well as others. It must be undertaken in a very conscious manner. The lack of consciousness is the cause of much failure in businesses.

When you choose to be self-employed, you are the creator. Your business will have a great deal of your personal creativity invested in it. This is a double-edged sword. We can actually stall our ability to manifest and/or impede the natural evolution of our business. When you embark on self-employment you have to support the flow of your creative energy. To do that effectively you have to be attuned to your emotional landscape, so that you don't inadvertently sabotage your own efforts. This Circle shows you how to begin to consciously address self-employment.

Circle Example: Establishing a Foundation for Self-Employment

North: Assess personal & spiritual impact

Northwest: Make changes to create balance

Northeast: Seek external perspective

West: Assess effects on what's around you

Center: Gaining the larger perspective

East: Establish the energetics

Southwest: Check energetics

Southeast: Research & resources

South: Develop business plan

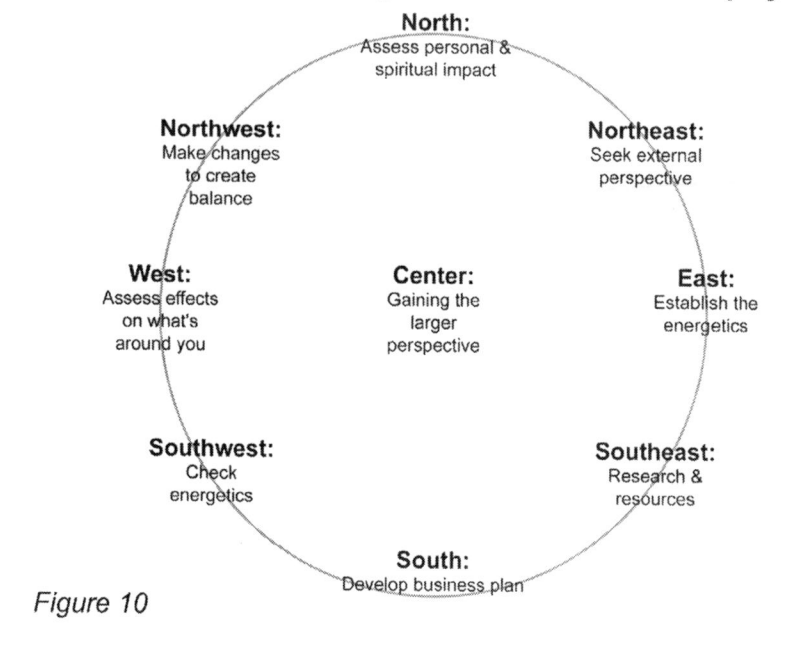

Figure 10

East (Beginning): Establish your foundational energetics – What makes a self-employment-based business sustainable? You must build the business on a strong energetic foundation from the beginning. If you do so, the business will sustain itself, and the results will be fulfilling. If you don't do this at the beginning, you're always going to have to put more and more energy into the business—otherwise, it will fold.

As a newly self-employed person, you establish the energetics by:

- **Getting clear emotionally** – By this we mean *acknowledging* what's present for you emotionally. For example, acknowledge that you're scared to death (if you are). If you're angry that there are rules and regulations you have to follow, and you're feeling rebellious with them, then acknowledge that, too. Identify any issues that trigger your emotions. For example, check in with yourself about your being solely responsible for the success or failure of your business. What emotions come up? Did your parents have expectations about what you would do for a living?

Acknowledging that those issues exist, as well as the triggers that set you off. Then, make a commitment not to react from that place. As a result of this process, you will be more resolved, and you will have a clearer starting point. Lack of emotional clarity is a major cause of business failure. This is necessary work that everyone, even leaders of larger corporations, should do.

- **Getting clear about your motivation** –Your inspiration is a large part of your business's foundation. You must be clear about why you are starting this business. The first question is: Is your motivation based in greed, or is it coming from love or passion? Remember that greed is not a sufficient motivator. If there is no love or passion, then greed won't carry you through, particularly if there are tough times. Also check in with yourself regarding whether your motivation to be self-employed is coming primarily

~ 206 ~

from *you*—or from someone else. For example, are you doing this because this is what your family wants, or because your father has always been self-employed? If the motivation is truly coming from you, then your likelihood of success is increased.

- **Letting go of investments in perfection** - Whenever we start something new we want to get it right, and we can be very critical of our own performance. You must let go of whether or not you're going to be flawless at this. Starting a business is a learning process, and there will be trials and errors. Small failures are part of the process. You must accept that, and embrace mistakes as opportunities for improving your business.

- **Setting your attitude** – Becoming self-employed is an adventure. Set that attitude for yourself, and commit to using it as a touchstone.

Southeast (Research and Resources) – Now, do your homework. Find out everything that's required to start your business. Look into all the logistics of setting up the business. This work is an essential part of creating the energetic support and root for your business. This work includes:

- **Market Research & Planning** – Here you ask all the necessary questions to help you understand and evaluate the potential in your chosen market. You'll address such questions as: What are the possibilities? Who will you serve? What do you know about them? Who is your competition? How will you reach your intended audience? How will you market and advertise? How will your ethics, morals, and boundaries influence the advertising process?

- **Paperwork Investigation** – What paperwork is required to set up your business? There's considerable paperwork to get accustomed to, and you want to be prepared with it.

Research all paperwork so you know specifically what is required, and when it must be submitted. For example, if you want to set up as a simple or limited liability corporation, what paperwork is required on local, state, and federal levels?

- **Supply Acquisition** - What provisions do you need to run your business? Determine what they are. Determine what may need acquiring or upgrading. Now, look at resources for supply acquisition. Determine your best sources, and set up those accounts. All of this has to be established before you begin to work, otherwise it will distract from productivity.

- **Research Profession-related Requirements & Resources** – What tools and techniques do you need to acquire to be really effective at your chosen work? Do you need any additional training or education? How will you acquire it? What investments are required? For example, if you are developing a business as a coach, you will need to research all the different resources (creative, academic, networking, etc.), that you will need to do the best possible job for your clients.

- **Set up Accounting** - How will you do accounting? Get acquainted with what's required, and set it up. Establish your accounting process in a way that's comfortable for you, so you don't fight with it. This is part of maintaining a good attitude.

South (The Actualization): Develop a Business Plan – Now, ask yourself, what steps do I need to take to make my business successful over what period of time? What is it I want to accomplish, and how do I want to accomplish it? This is where you develop your plan of action. A business plan has specific components, and there are many resources that delineate those for you. Plan exactly *what you're going to do,* and exactly *how you're* *doing to do it.* Note that you want to create a program you can stick with. It needs to be comfortable for you, and that you can realistically do it.

Southwest (Test & Adjust): Check your energetics – At this point you need to do a personal assessment of the energetics you set up in the East. Check in with yourself in regard to your:

- **Emotional clarity** – How are you doing in terms of remaining clear and steady vs. reacting emotionally? Is there more work for you to do?
- **Motivational energy** – Is your motivation still strong and grounded in love and/or passion?
- **Investments** – What are you invested in that you need to let go of?
- **Attitude** –Have you been able to maintain a good attitude?

West (Assess & Evaluate): Evaluate the Impact on What's Around You – Now, step back from your personal assessment, and evaluate the effect of this particular work on the important externals, such as:

- Your immediate family and home environment
- Your extended family and that environment
- Your friends and community

Then, step back and look at the larger circle so you have some sense of what you're getting into. For example, will your work affect the politics of the area? Will it affect the economy? Will it affect the environment? Always assess what your effect is and, in particular, look to see whether there is any adverse effect on all that is around you.

NW (Balance): Implement Changes to Create Balance – Based on your two sets of assessments, you know what needs to change. Now, make those changes. Make adjustments to both your business plan and to your personal energetics. This is an action-oriented point.

North (Commitment & Equilibrium): Assess Personal and Spiritual Impact - Here, you perform an evaluation on how your business is affecting you personally and spiritually. To do this assessment you need to ask deep spiritual, moral, and ethical questions. For example, you may ask yourself:

- Is anything about my business creating any moral or ethical problems for me?
- Is this business breaking any of my personal boundaries, or creating boundary problems of any sort?
- Am I looking at what it takes to maintain a balance of my emotions, my physical presentation, etc., etc.?

If you're trying to use Universal Laws and Principles as the main structure of your business, then you have to ask:

- Am I truly following those guidelines?
- Am I making altruistic decisions?

This assessment is difficult for a lot of people. You may have to acknowledge that you've done things that were not in keeping with these values. You may have to acknowledge being greedy, or even ruthless. If so, you have to ask yourself whether you intend to keep doing so, regardless of harm to self or others. Once you acknowledge what you have done in the past and resolve to act differently in the future, you can release it. While difficult, this assessment brings you into a state of equilibrium, inner peace, and strength. By not doing this, you can create inner turmoil that will come back to haunt you later.

Northeast (Complete & Prepare): Seek External Perspective –It's now time to seek out a trusted source who can give you honest and substantive feedback on your plans and on what you've accomplished so far. It is best if you consolidate this into one package that you can hand over to this individual or group. You want good, thoughtful, and insightful input that will tell you what you're not seeing (i.e., your blind spots), and can give you solid advice and counsel.

Return to the East: You want to return to the East to begin again and re-establish your energetics, based on all that you have learned in this first cycle.

Center (The Big Picture) – Now, you go the Center. It is here that you integrate all the information you've accumulated through this circular process. Take your time to assess and assimilate this knowledge, then you may go to the next level, which is the actualization circle.

Circle Example: Start-Up of a Profit-Making Business (Manufacturing)

Circle Example: Start-Up of a Profit-Making Business (Manufacturing)

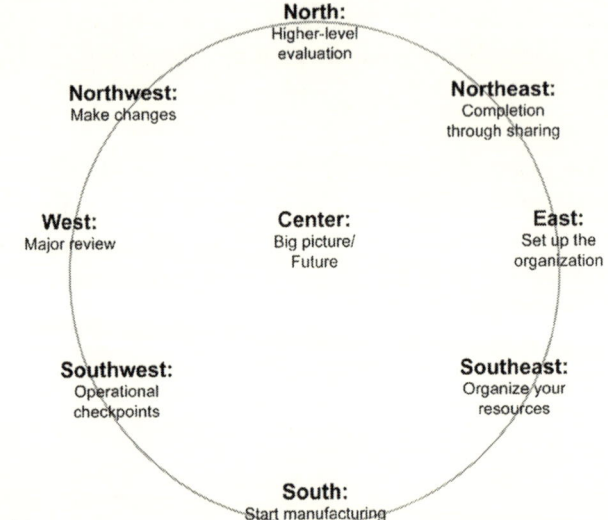

- **North:** Higher-level evaluation
- **Northeast:** Completion through sharing
- **East:** Set up the organization
- **Southeast:** Organize your resources
- **South:** Start manufacturing
- **Southwest:** Operational checkpoints
- **West:** Major review
- **Northwest:** Make changes
- **Center:** Big picture/Future

Figure 11

East (Starting Place) – Set up your business organization in accordance with your business plan: articles of incorporation, tax identification, etc. Establish your Board of Directors.

SE (Organize Resources) – Hire personnel, do budget, line up material sources, set up personnel plans, and organize management and major departments.

South (Work) – Start up the manufacturing process.

SW (Operational Checkpoints) – The focus here is on doing an operational evaluation. You'll want to assess and refine such things as production levels, employee productivity, material flow, employee benefits, etc. This should occur simultaneously with the South work. As you start up your manufacturing process also begin your process of checking and adjusting.

West (Major Review)– Do an overall evaluation of everything: the Board of Directors, how you're presenting yourself, your workforce, production levels, administration efficiency, etc.

NW (Make Changes) – Implement changes identified in West.

North (Higher-Level Review) –Take your review to a higher-level and evaluate your organization's performance in terms of your ideals, values, and original vision. You created a manufacturing process to serve certain needs. Revisit those needs. Are they still relevant? Look at the overall purpose, or mission of your organization. Is it still vital? What is the state of your workforce's morale?

NE (Completion by Sharing) – Close this cycle by sharing with your personnel and the community around you. Are there: profits to be shared? What can you do to thank and benefit the larger community? What can you do to replenish the natural resources and environment?

Center (Big Picture Evaluation/Evolution) –What is your Vision of the future? What will that vision accomplish? What would be the long-term effects and ramifications of achieving it? What will it take to bring it about?

Author Biographies

Tu Moonwalker is of Apache and So. American Native American heritage and has been teaching spirituality for over 20 years, focusing on bringing sacredness into our daily lives.

Tu has also been active in the business world all of her adult life, and has explored how to practice sacredness in all those varied experiences. She has worked as an executive secretary, office manager, chef, and as a consultant to museums. She has run her own successful art business, help found several non-profit organizations, and has sat on or chaired several Boards of Directors for both profit and non-profit organizations.

She has also done formal studies in both spiritual and academic realms. Tu holds two bachelor degrees and two masters degrees. She is a Master with Circle Knowledge, a Grand Master Wisdom Holder and is co-founder of a serious system of spiritual study as well as an active Canon-minister.

Tu is now an active business consultant, singing/voice coach, spiritual mentor/counselor, and artist/craftswoman. She is included in *Who's Who of America*, *Who's Who of American Women*, and *Who's Who in the World*.

JoAnne O'Brien-Levin, Ph.D., has a deep commitment to the development of both individuals and organizations. She has worked as a writer, instructional designer, media producer, organizational development consultant, and personal coach.

JoAnne was nationally recognized for her work as an innovative, award-winning designer of interactive training and did pioneering work in the field of organizational learning. She collaborated with business executives to co-author a book, *The Power of Collaborative Leadership: Lessons for the Learning Organization*. In the book's foreword, Peter Senge writes that it is a "rare book...(that) delves deeply to explore non-trivial insights and potential guiding principles that emerge from experience."

Her intellectual training includes a doctorate from the Annenberg School for Communication at USC. During the past decade JoAnne has dedicated herself to learning how indigenous wisdom can contribute to the transformation of our culture.

Láné Saán Moonwalker is a spiritual teacher and healer of Yaqui and Jewish heritage. Lané's parents were activists who helped many people of all backgrounds establish themselves and start successful business ventures, co-founding a center in Denver for that purpose. While growing up she was also privileged to learn the healing arts from members of her family who were both highly skilled *curenderas* (i.e., traditional healers who combine Native and Catholic spiritual beliefs and practices*)*.

Lané absorbed her parent's political, worldly and business acumen and, over time, interwove it with her spiritual practice such that the two cannot be separated. Lané sees the spiritual and the practical as partners. She teaches, consults, and counsels from that place of wholeness.

Lané has studied with many spiritual teachers, including artist, writer, and visionary Joseph Rael (a.k.a., Beautiful Painted Arrow), Rev. Marian Starnes, and EricTao. Lané is an accomplished artist, a weaver and painter, as well as a dancer and singer, and holds a degree in humanities and the visual arts from the University of Colorado. She has been a licensed minister for more than two decades.

Endnotes

[1] Wendell Berry in "The Road and the Wheel" from *A Continuous Harmony: Essays Cultural and Agricultural* (Harcourt Brace Jovanovich, 1972), p. 140.

[2] To do the job most effectively, we should attempt to investigate "all sides" of an issue equally. However, if we look at what actually tends to happen, we see that we often gather information that only supports one point of view. Furthermore, we may focus on, even validate, only certain *types* of information while dismissing other types. For example, Western culture tends to focus on intellectual information at the expense of other kinds. That information is primarily consumed in audiovisual form, a communication form that has some intrinsic limitations. The result of this tendency is that we are effectively narrowing our perceptive capabilities. Because we are narrowing our perceptive capacity, we are also narrowing our diagnostic abilities. As a result, our foundations are weak, and we lack the capacity to truly understand the nature of the problems we encounter. This is not an effective approach. Some of this is attributable to the nature of the line in conjunction with the square.

[3] When we frame an argument or take a photograph, we use the square blueprint to focus on a single perspective, moment, or aspect of the whole. In so doing, however, we leave something out. In fact, we leave a lot out. For that is the nature of the square.

[4] For more on Mandalas, see the Wikipedia:
http://en.wikipedia.org/wiki/Mandala

[5] Joseph Campbell's *The Power of Myth* (NY: Doubleday Press, 1988), p. 109.

[6] See *The Discovery of the Circle* by Bruno Munari (G. Wittenborn, 1965), p. 62.

[7] We are indebted to *Man and His Symbols* by Carl G. Jung and M.-L. von Franz, Joseph L. Henderson, Jolande Jacobi, and Aniela Jaffé (Aldus Books, 1964). For more on the role of circles in human culture please see pp. 266-285 of that volume.

[8] *A History of the Circle: Mathematical Reasoning and the Physical Universe* by Ernest Zebrowski (Rutgers U. Press, 2000), pp. 26-7.

[9] Also, from *The Discovery of the Circle*, p. 65.

[10] From *Black Elk Speaks* by John Neihardt (Bison Books, 2004).

[11] "For the nomadic peoples of the North American prairie the tipi expressed their connection to the universe. Its circular ground plan echoed not only the larger atmospheric circle, but also the encompassing disk of the earth, stretched out beneath the heavens. The floor represented the earth and the walls the sky; the poles were the pathways between the two realms, linking the human inhabitants to *Wakan Tanka*, the Great Mystery above... The very act of building (a tipi) was at the same time a means of comprehending the universe as well as an acceptance of one's place in the cosmic order." Source: "Dwellings as metaphor for the worldview of the community," in *The Spirit Word*, Time-Life, Alexandria, VA, 1992.

[12] For more on this topic, see Dr. David Ulansey's website: http://www.well.com/user/davidu/extinction.ht

[13] For more on Agnes Baker Pilgrim, please see: http://www.agnesbakerpilgrim.org/

[14] What is the difference between a law and a principle?
- A Universal Law is a description of some aspect of energy within Universal Flow that just "is." We don't know its origin; it is beyond our knowing. We understand through observation, experience of interactions, or by processes that are constantly being supported by synchronicity, that it's so.
- Principles are supportive of Universal Laws. They are the bridgework; they are stepping stones that help us understand and work with a Universal Law. For example, the Universal Law of Chaos has many principles below it, including Acceptance. By practicing acceptance during chaotic situations we learn to work with the Universal Law of Chaos.

[15] In the past, anthropologists have used the term "reciprocity" to try to capture the practice of exchange they saw being actively practiced amongst native peoples. In time, the term became associated with more sensational activities that were not in keeping with the original intention of the practice. The anthropologists failed to grasp the deeper meaning of the principle that the natives were trying to work with. The natives were trying to work with the Principle of Equitable Exchange. It's the true meaning of this principle that deserves our attention.

[16] Historically, each nation had a specific orientation to the Circle. This orientation was dependent upon a variety of factors, including the geographical and historical location of a particular group within a larger community, nation, or confederation. This orientation would determine where the Circle began, and

therefore the direction from which they entered the circle. For example, the Iroquois entered from the North. Others, such as the Apache and the Cheyenne, would enter from the East. The majority entered from the East, and that is why we have oriented our representation of the Circle in this manner.

[17] The Circle encompasses all the modalities articulated by noted psychologist Carl Jung: thinking, feeling, sensing, intuition. (In fact, Jung often presented these four functions in a circular form, corresponding to the Cardinal directions.)

[18] Because there is constant movement in the Circle, there is constant change in the Circle's beingness. So it's constantly changing—and so are we; we're just not conscious of it. Our physical vessel is, in fact, in constant change. If we would just be in touch with the Circle and its beingness, and the beingness of our own physical vessel, we would be more comfortable with constant change—including rapid constant change.

[19] Critics of globalization in its current form include environmentalists and trade-unionists. Some of the negative impacts they point to include:
- Globalization operates mostly in the interests of the richest countries, at the expense of developing countries. The role of developing countries in the world market is mostly to provide the North and West with cheap labor and raw materials.
- Local communities are often disrupted. Multinational companies (MNCs), with their vast economies of scale, may drive local companies out of business. In addition, profits may not benefit local communities; they are sent back to where the MNC is based. If it becomes cheaper to operate in another country the MNC is likely to pull up stakes, which disrupts that community.
- International laws may be not be sufficiently strict or well-enforced, meaning that MNCs may operate in harmful ways such as polluting the environment, running risks with safety, or imposing poor working conditions and low wages on local workers.
- The world's cultural diversity is threatened when local economies, traditions and languages languish, or are overrun by Western culture.

For more information, please see:http://www.bbc.co.uk/schools/gcsebitesize/geography/economic/globalisationrev5.shtml

[20] See *Blessed Unrest: How the Largest Movement in the World Came into Being and Why No One Saw it Coming,* by Paul Hawken (Viking: 2007), p. 125.

[21] See Hawken, p. 125.

[22] "Characteristic of the linear vision," wrote Wendell Berry in *A Continuous Harmony*," is the idea that anything is justifiable in so far as it's immediately good for something else." Only if it proves to be good *for* something are we then ready to say that it's worth something, that it has *value*, by which of course we mean money. That is also why "any organism that is not contributing obviously and directly to the workings of the economy is now endangered—which means…that (even) human society is endangered." In contrast, when humans live in accordance with the Circle we are "more accepting of mystery and more humble." It assumes that all things have a use, but recognizes that humans have limited perception, and therefore cannot judge what those uses are. Therefore, when we live in accordance with the Circle, all things are valued—not for their use, but for their own sake. They are a part of the larger, sacred whole, and thus worthy of our respect.

[23] For more on this topic, please see the documentary film, *The Corporation*, and/or the book: *The Corporation: The Pathological Pursuit of Profit and Power* by Joel Bakan. More information is available on this website: http://www.thecorporation.com/index.cfm

[24] The linear vision sees man as moving through time in a linear fashion. This is what Wendell Berry calls "the doctrine of progress." Because the line only moves forward, we experience life as if everything were happening for the first time. We discard old experience as we encounter new. "But when the new is assumed to be a constant," Berry continues, "discipline fails, for discipline is preparation, and the new cannot be prepared for; it cannot, in any very meaningful way, be expected…(W)e therefore having nothing to learn from our elders, nothing to teach our children. Civilization is thus reduced to a sequence of last-minute improvisations, desperately building today out of the wreckage of yesterday." From "The Road and the Wheel" in *A Continuous Harmony: Essays Cultural and Agricultural* by Wendell Berry (Harcourt Brace Jovanovich, 1972), p. 139-140.

Printed in the United Kingdom by
Lightning Source UK Ltd., Milton Keynes
138620UK00002BA/4/P